Playing in the Kitchen

Recipes, Stories and Explorations to Feed the Whole Self

Lavinia Plonka

m a v e n

Maven

Asheville, NC

ISBN 978-0-557-03275-4

Cover and Author Photos: Ron Morecraft

Book Design: Jack Rizzo

This book is dedicated

to Lidia and Leo Plonka,

who taught me that food,

like life, is to be savored.

Contents

Salads and Side Dishes

INTRODUCTION

Non-cooks think it's silly to invest two hours' work in two minutes' enjoyment;
but if cooking is evanescent, so is the ballet.

— Julia Child

I owe my approach to cooking to a seminal childhood event. My mother seemed like a wizard in the kitchen. I would sit on the stool and watch, fascinated. Occasionally she allowed me to do little things, like stir or pour. It was very exciting. One day, when I was about 9, they did something no parent in 21st century America would dream of. They went out to run errands and left me alone with my two younger siblings. I decided, since my parents worked so hard, that I would surprise them by making soup. I put everything I loved into my soup; potatoes, noodles, barley and salt. I gave it a stir, and then went outside to play, because I knew soup cooks itself. When my parents pulled into the driveway a couple of hours later, I could hardly wait to show them the surprise. Unbelievably, my brilliant soup had cooked down into a charred pot of inedible paste. My parents, who were generally harsh disciplinarians, laughed and congratulated me on trying something so difficult. My mother explained the nature of starch. And my father said, "The important thing is that you tried something new. Nothing ventured, nothing gained!"

These words have informed most of my life choices, but never more than in the kitchen. While there have been some spectacular failures in my culinary adventures, fortunately, no one's survival depended on it. The only suffering that occurred was my bruised ego. And unlike a failed career or marriage, it's quite simple to just start over. I can't tell you how many times the word "Oops!" has escaped my lips – whether it's because a carrot leapt from the chopping board and landed in the compost bucket, or because I just thoughtlessly dumped the chocolate into the food processor that I was supposed to carefully fold in at the end of a recipe. I have accidentally skipped steps in a recipe, omitted entire sections and misread the directions. I have botched my share of mayonnaises and sponge cakes. But I've also discovered some really cool recipe variations, developed new approaches to a recipe and sometimes ended up revamping a recipe entirely because my error opened up new possibilities.

Throughout my lifetime of playing in the kitchen, I have been a passionate student of personal development. My first career as a performer was dedicated to creating and performing stories of search and transformation (with the help of some slapstick comedy). This led to a curiosity about the nature of our emotions and expressions. I discovered the Feldenkrais Method of Somatic Education. Somatic Education is literally educating through the body. As a practitioner of this elegant approach to self study (Smithsonian Magazine once called it a "revolutionary approach to learning"), I began to recognize the links between habitual tensions, our emotional life and how we get in our own way. This led to two of my books: *What Are You Afraid Of? A Body/Mind Guide to Courageous Living* and *Walking Your Talk: Changing Your Life through the Magic of Body Language*.

This study of the relationship of movement to tension spilled over into other aspects of life, including the kitchen. I noticed how some people get nervous at the thought of cooking. Whether due to upbringing, temperament or lack of experience, the idea of play does not enter into their culinary experience. Cooking is a chore, or even a terrifying event. Some people spend huge amounts of money on catered meals in fear of disappointing their guests with their own attempts. I've seen cooks chop with their shoulders up by their ears, grim determination wiring their jaws into grimaces of pain. I found myself devising exercises for my friends to help with better body mechanics or relaxation as we prepared meals together. Then some chefs came to see me for Feldenkrais lessons because of repetitive strain injuries or aching feet. I began to be curious about the connection between playing in the kitchen and relaxation.

Meanwhile, people who knew my love of cooking started asking me for recipes. At one point I compiled them into a booklet. Requests increased. People complained that their booklet fell apart or that the food stains had made the ink run. Publications began requesting humorous articles about food and the body. And suddenly, all of this material seemed to call for what you are holding in your hand. Recipes, stories, movement exercises for better use of self and tips for transforming cooking from work to play are the ingredients of this literary buffet I've prepared for you.

Playing in the kitchen can be a metaphoric journey, a body/mind investigation or just the act of baking a pie. Therefore, I'm offering a smorgasbord of options for exploring your personal relationship to kitchen playtime. Here's the menu.

Recipes

I cannot take credit for most of the recipes. I have culled them from books, magazines, NPR stories, old wives' tales and the occasional flash of personal brilliance. While many of the sources are out of print, when it seems appropriate or useful, I have included the source for your further reading. The recipes I've chosen are not designed to teach you how to cook, or how to cook in a particular style. They are the recipes people always ask me about. They are the recipes I've mailed and emailed to others so many times they live in a special file. I have made so many mistakes cooking most of these recipes, that I've discovered variations, or at least have learned ways to rescue the meal. Therefore every recipe also contains tips, suggestions, and "rescue remedies" such as substitutions for missing ingredients so that meal preparation can remain play and not turn into a hair-raising exploit.

Explorations

I have been a teacher of the Feldenkrais Method for many years. Dr. Moshe Feldenkrais was an engineer, martial artist and athlete who developed a movement technology that affords anyone the opportunity to live a more functional, pain-free life. Using sequences of small movements, the Feldenkrais Method teaches us how to use ourselves more effectively. It is used in universities and rehab clinics around the world. People at all levels of performance, from Olympic athletes and concert violinists to persons suffering from limitations due to injury or illness, attest to its value for increasing abilities and enhancing quality of life. The Felenkrais Method allows you to discover, in a delightful and effortless manner, how to free yourself of lifelong habits of tension and holding.

I have included several movement explorations based on Feldenkrais' teachings that I have found particularly helpful not just in the kitchen, but in all aspects of life. Some of them are designed to be done before or after cooking, but most can just be integrated into your kitchen routine. They can reduce stress, ease physical and mental discomfort and improve use of self while chopping, cooking or even lifting heavy pots. Since it's not easy to work in the kitchen and read movement instructions at the same time, I have recorded the explorations in this book. They are available as free audio downloads on my website: www.laviniaplonka.com. Play them while you're playing in the kitchen!

Stories

I've included stories about food, about cooking food, about my relationship to food. Some of them are traditional folk tales that I have found particularly relevant. Some of them are essays from my own never ending relationship with the act

10

of cooking.

So if you never cook a single recipe from this book, I hope you will find some of the other ingredients I've included worth tasting. Words are as much a feast for the mind as food is for the body. Above all, I hope that this book inspires a sense of play – in the kitchen and in life.

Bon Appétit!

About the "Playing With Your Food" Section:

In speaking with many people, I've narrowed down the biggest obstacles to a sense of play while cooking.

1. Worrying about what meals work for guests
2. Missing an ingredient and fearing substitution
3. What happens if I miss a step or mix up the order in a recipe – oops!
4. The danger of burning down the kitchen
5. Concern that no one will like the food

Therefore, at the end of each recipe, I have included a section that offers suggestions for easing any stress during preparation.

Playing With Your Food

Guests:
This will tell you whether this is a good party recipe, or warnings about complications when multiplying.

Substitutions:
This will give you ideas of ways to vary the meal based on ingredients you forgot to buy, things you'd like to add, or ways to get around a missing item.

Oops:
Here I will describe things I've done wrong and how you can avoid them, or repair any damage.

Fire:

This is a heads up for an incendiary potential in the recipe – flashpoints, burning possibilities, overcooking, etc.

You notice that the box does not contain Issue #5: No one will like it. It's a fact of life that if you try to please everyone, you end up pleasing no one, so the important thing in cooking is to please yourself. The recipes included in this book come from a lifetime of collecting, trying, tasting, failing and trying again. In order to qualify for inclusion in this book, someone at some point in my life either begged me for the recipe, told me it belonged in a book (which is usually where I got it!) or asked me to bring that dish to an event. So I invite you to let that fear go.

A Note about exotic names and tastes:

As we move toward a global society, many things that seemed exotic twenty years ago have become standard fare. Hummus was once confused with dirt. Yogurt was considered the province of "hippies," and is now in every child's lunch box. There are dishes and ingredients in this book that come from a variety of cultures, as well as comfortable standards. I have translated or explained any dishes with exotic names. Any ingredient that seems unusual or foreign I have starred with an asterisk. These ingredients are listed in the glossary in the back of the book. I have also included some online sources for purchase, although most ingredients can be found in local gourmet stores. Soon, they will become staples in your kitchen.

APPETIZERS

Our minds are like our stomachs; they are whetted by the change of their food,
and variety supplies both with fresh appetites.
— Quintilian

Finding Your Center

Any beginning is auspicious: the beginning of a dinner party, a family meal, or your quiet meal alone. The "little something" before dinner can create a sense of anticipation and atmosphere.

You can make the beginning of meal preparation equally special. Like an athlete warming up, or a yogi beginning with chanting "ohm", there are ways to prepare the mind and body for fun in the kitchen. You could consider it an "appetizer" to your culinary process. That would of course, make washing dishes your dessert – but more on that later.

Here is a little exercise you can try before cooking, or before any activity. It can help you find the pleasure and ease in your posture and attitude as you work.

Stand for a moment with your eyes closed. Sense the movement of your breath in your abdomen. You can even put your hand there to feel the movement. Tune your awareness to a spot about 1 ½ inches below your belly button. This is what in

Asian tradition is called the Dantien,Tanden or the Hara. Often Westerners call it the core. This is your power center. Now draw an imaginary line from your Tanden point down your right leg. Draw another one down your left leg. Draw a third line from the Tanden up your back into your head. Try to keep these lines in your awareness as you breathe. Now, notice your face. Imagine the outer corners of your mouth moving outward towards your ears. Just imagine what your face would feel like, without actually doing it. Keep your attention on your Tanden and your breath as you imagine. Slowly open your eyes.

Each time you start to feel stressed as you cook, use this little exercise as a way to bring you back in touch with your center and your personal joy. Your "inner smile" is there any time you close your eyes and sense your center.

Saté or Satay

(Basically means marinated, grilled meat on a stick – perhaps of Indonesian origin but no one knows)

Serves 4 - 8

8 or more 8-inch bamboo skewers

8 – 16 oz. tempeh* or boneless chicken

2 tablespoons lime juice

2 teaspoons vegetable oil

1/4 teaspoon salt

Preheat grill or broiler. Soak the skewers for at least 15 minutes.

Tempeh version:

Slice tempeh into 1x4 -inch "fingers" and slide them lengthwise on skewer. Mix remaining ingredients and baste as you grill, turning occasionally until brown.

Chicken Version:

Cut the chicken into bite size pieces or strips that are slightly shorter than the skewer. If you have time, marinate the chicken pieces in the lime mixture, and make another batch of lime for basting. But if you're pressed for time, just basting is fine. Place 3 or 4 pieces on a skewer or thread the skewer through one long strip. Cook as above.

Serve with either Peanut Sauce or Sambal Tomat (see below)

Sauces for Saté
Hot and Tangy Peanut Sauce
Makes about 3/4 cup

This works as a quick saté sauce, or is excellent on any kind of Chinese noodles. This sauce is great if you are serving tempeh to people who are afraid of foods that are not made out of meat. It thickens as it stands and can be thinned with coconut milk, lime juice or water.

1/4 cup chunky peanut butter
1/4 cup coconut milk (either regular or low fat)
3 tablespoons lime juice
2 tablespoons coarsely chopped cilantro (including stems) or basil leaves
1 tablespoon soy sauce
2 teaspoons brown sugar
1 clove garlic - peeled
1/4 teaspoon red pepper flakes

Place all in food processor, blend till smooth. If it looks too thick, add a few drops of water. Will last a week tightly covered in refrigerator.

Sambal Tomat

(Indonesian Spicy Tomato Sauce)

Makes about 1 1/2 cups.

2 teaspoons vegetable oil

2 tablespoons minced shallots

2 teaspoons peeled, minced fresh ginger root (see note below)

2 cloves minced garlic

Pinch red pepper flakes

1 1/2 cups chopped tomatoes

1 teaspoon brown sugar

2 whole chili peppers (any variety), halved and seeded

1 -2 tablespoons lime juice

Salt to taste

1/4 cup minced green onion (scallions)

Note: The best way to peel ginger is to use a vegetable peeler. Peel approximately the amount you want before you cut it off the main root. That way you have something to grip.

Heat oil in skillet or wok; stir fry shallot, ginger, garlic and red pepper flakes over medium heat, one minute. Add tomatoes, sugar and chilies, cook over medium low heat, five - eight minutes or until tomato softens and begins to give off juice. Remove from heat. For a less fiery sauce, remove and discard chilies. Place cooked tomato mixture in blender or food processor. Add lime juice and process until almost smooth. Pour into small serving bowl; salt to taste. Garnish with green onions. Let cool before serving.

Playing With Your Food

Guests:

The amount of sauce is enough to serve 8 people, so adjust your tempeh/chicken amounts higher or lower depending on how many you are serving.

Substitution:

Got no lime? Use lemon.

Don't have brown sugar? Use maple syrup, honey or even regular sugar.

No red pepper flakes? Add a touch of hot sauce or cayenne. No chilies? Skip it. Only smooth peanut butter? It's fine.

Oops!:

If you accidentally throw everything for the Sambal Tomat into the frying pan at once, it might be a little less flavorful, but not a disaster.

Fire:

If you don't soak the bamboo skewers, you may get some charring, but I know people who don't care.

If you don't check the broiling food, it could scorch, but you'll smell it before you're in danger.

Stuffed Endive Leaves

Makes about 20 portions

8 ounces firm or extra firm silken tofu*

1/4 cup white miso*

2 tablespoons rice vinegar

2 tablespoons safflower, peanut or sesame oil. (See note)

1 clove garlic, finely minced or pressed

3 tablespoons minced onion

1/2 cup minced red bell pepper

1/2 cup minced celery

20 Belgian endive leaves

20 sprigs watercress or parsley

Note: It's not easy to find untoasted sesame oil. If you use toasted sesame oil, it will have an extremely strong flavor, so use only one tablespoon along with a tablespoon of some more neutral oil like safflower or canola.

Put the tofu in a pot and pour boiling water over it, enough to cover it; then put a lid on the pot. Let it sit about five minutes, then rinse the tofu under cold water, enough to cool. Wrap the tofu in cheesecloth or a porous dish cloth and squeeze out the water. The more water you squeeze out, the more solid your stuffing will be. You may actually find you need more than one cloth to absorb all the water. While it's OK to have a little moisture, the more you can squeeze out of it (it's kind of fun and sensual), the firmer your filling will be.

Place the first five ingredients into a food processor or blender and blend until smooth. Mix in the onion, bell pepper and celery. Refrigerate for at least two hours to let the flavors develop. This spread can be made 1 - 2 days in advance if kept covered and chilled, making it great for party preparation. When you're ready to serve, place a heaping teaspoon of the spread on the lower half of each endive leaf. Tuck a sprig of watercress or parsley into the spread as a garnish. Arrange on a platter.

Playing With Your Food

Guests:
This is a simple, gorgeous and delicious dish for parties

Substitutions:
white wine vinegar can work instead of rice vinegar

Oops!:
I once threw the onions into the blender – makes for a watery spread, but still tasty.

Cold Sesame Noodles
Serves 4

16 oz package noodles (soba, udon, or Chinese, they all work)

1/4 cup tahini*

2 tablespoons peanut butter

1/2 cup brewed black tea

2 cloves garlic, minced or crushed through garlic press

2 tablespoons toasted sesame oil

1 tablespoon rice vinegar

2 tablespoons tamari or soy sauce

1 teaspoon hot chili oil

1 teaspoon sugar, honey or other sweetener

Optional Garnish:

Peeled shredded cucumber and/or finely chopped scallions

Toasted sesame seeds

Prepare noodles according to package directions. Allow to cool – if you keep them in cold water, they won't stick together. I have made this dish many times where the noodles were still warm – tastes great.

Mix together tahini, peanut butter, garlic, sesame oil, vinegar, tamari, hot chili oil and sweetener. Add tea a little at a time, till the sauce is at the thickness you like. Usually it's less than 1/2 cup. Pour over noodles and toss well. Garnish as desired. Add more tamari and chili oil to taste.

Playing With Your Food

Guests:
People love this; however, if the noodles sit around too long, they might get a little stiff. If that happens, add some peanut oil and re-toss.

Substitution:
Any noodle will do, I've even used linguini.
They are fine without any garnish.
I've left out the peanut butter, used white wine vinegar instead of rice vinegar, cayenne instead of chili oil, just for a few suggestions.

Oops!:
I have accidentally poured in all the tea at once – it made it a little thin, I just thickened it with some more tahini and refrigerated the extra.

The Red Peppers
Russian Tale

There was once a poor, simple Mountaineer whose wife sent him to the village to get some supplies. He was dazzled by all the wonderful things that everyone was selling, but fearing a hiding from his wife, bought only the things she had re-

Roast the peppers over a gas flame, under a broiler or on a grill, turning until blackened and blistered all over. Place in a bag – plastic or paper – for ten minutes. This loosens the skin, which should peel off easily. After peeling, slit the peppers open and remove the membranes, stems and seeds. Allow them to drain.

Meanwhile, combine the walnuts and breadcrumbs in a food processor and process until finely ground. Add the peppers, lemon juice and pomegranate molasses and blend until creamy. Add the chili paste to taste, adjust the seasoning and scrape into a jar or container with a tight lid. Chill overnight and allow flavors to mellow.

To serve, scrape dip into a serving dish, decorate with ground cumin and a drizzle of olive oil. Serve with pita bread or crackers.

Playing With Your Food

Guests:
You can make this dish up to five days ahead of time; in fact, it tastes even better after sitting at least one day. That way you're not preparing all the party food on the day of the event.

Substitutions:
Pomegranate molasses are not always easy to find. You can skip it and it will be a perfectly fine dip. You can add more lemon and a touch of honey if you want that "tang". Every Middle Eastern book I consulted has a different recipe for this dip – I even read one that had no red peppers, just some cayenne added to the walnuts!

Oops!:
I once threw the peppers into the food processor with the bread crumbs and walnuts – no harm done.

Fire:
Keep your eye on the peppers, after an initial wait, they blacken quickly.

Hummus

Yield about 3 cups

2 cups cooked chick peas, drained, with reserved cooking liquid.

1 -3 cloves garlic, peeled (according to your love of garlic)

1/4 cup tahini

Juice of half a lemon

Salt and pepper

1/4 cup olive or vegetable oil

Purée the garlic cloves in the food processor, or crush them in a garlic press into the processor. Add chick peas, tahini, lemon juice, salt and pepper. If you are using canned chick peas, hold off on the salt till after you process. Slowly pour in the olive oil. Add cooking or can water to thin it out as much as you need to after the initial processing. You may want to add more olive oil as you process to make it creamier. Salt and pepper to taste. Serve with pita bread or crackers.

Playing With Your Food

Guests:
Somehow, people always make too much hummus. This recipe is plenty for an appetizer.

Substitution:
Some Greek recipes don't use tahini. Many people don't use olive oil, although that's what makes it richer tasting. And of course, you can add all kinds of things – red peppers, scallions, parsley. Chick peas seem to be the only consistent ingredient.

Oops!:
I've sometimes thoughtlessly thrown the whole garlic cloves in with the chick peas.

The danger of that is that it doesn't get fully processed, so someone would end up with a chunk of garlic. But if you process long enough, it should get absorbed.

Baba Ghanoush
(Middle Eastern Eggplant Dip)
Makes about 1 - 1 ½ cups

1 medium size eggplant
1 -2 cloves garlic, peeled
1/4 cup tahini
Juice of half a lemon
Salt

Turn broiler on high. Prick eggplant with fork all over. Place near broiler top, with aluminum foil in a pan on the rack below to catch the juices. Broil until soft and skin is charred – you need to keep turning it till the whole thing is black and the eggplant is soft and mushy to the touch. Remove from oven and let cool till you can handle it. Another great way to cook it is on the grill till the skin is black and the flesh is soft.

Allow it to cool enough to handle it. Meanwhile, purée garlic in food processor, or crush in garlic press and add it to the processor. Scrape eggplant pulp out of skin and place in food processor. Add other ingredients and process till smooth. Adjust the seasonings to your taste.

Playing With Your Food

Guests:
One eggplant is just about enough for 3 –4 people. So for a party, you really need to increase your amounts.

Fire:
You need to pay attention to the eggplant and turn it regularly. But the nice thing is that if it's charred, it's good.

Indian Eggplant Purée with Seasoned Yogurt

(adapted from Lord Krishna's Cuisine)

Serves 4 entrée, 6 appetizer

This is a great alternative to the old standby Baba Ghanoush. Serve it with Nan, an Indian bread, or you can use pita.

1 medium size eggplant

2 tablespoons Ghee* or vegetable oil

1 -2 teaspoons hot green chilies or jalapeños. seeded and minced.

1/8 teaspoon asafetida powder*

1 teaspoon cumin seeds

1 teaspoon ground coriander

1 teaspoon salt

2 tablespoons each finely chopped cilantro and mint

2/3 cup plain yogurt or sour cream

1 teaspoon garam masala*

Broil eggplant according to directions for Baba Ghanoush in the previous recipe. Scoop out the pulp. Discard the skin. Heat the ghee or oil in a large nonstick frying pan over moderate heat. When it is hot, but not smoking, add the green chilies, asafetida and cumin seeds and fry until the cumin seeds darken. Add the eggplant, ground coriander and salt, and cook, stirring frequently, until the mixture is dry and thick, about 10 minutes.

Remove the pan from the heat and let cool to room temperature. Stir in the fresh herbs, yogurt or sour cream and garam masala. Serve hot, at room temperature or cold.

Playing With Your Food

Substitution:

You can skip the asafetida

Use cumin powder instead of cumin seeds; just add them when you add the coriander.

If you don't have green chilies, use red, or even a dash of cayenne

Fire:

See eggplant note on pg. 25

Citrus Noodles

Serves 4 - 10

2 tablespoons dry sherry

1 tablespoon finely minced garlic

2 tablespoons olive oil

2 tablespoons soy sauce

2 tablespoons rice vinegar

2 tablespoons toasted sesame oil

1 tablespoon light brown sugar

1/2 tablespoon chili sauce

1/4 teaspoon Szechuan peppercorns

Zest of 1 lemon (see note)

1 green onion (also known as scallions)

1 - 2 packages noodles (Soba, Udon, or rice noodles)

Note: When making the lemon zest, place a piece of wax paper between the grater and the lemon. With your first few strokes, the grater pokes through the wax paper. Your lemon zest collects on the wax paper. You just brush it off and clean up is a breeze! When you grate, avoid getting too much white pith into your zest, it creates a bitter flavor.

Prepare noodles according to package directions. Sauté garlic and onion in olive oil until just before garlic browns. Add remaining ingredients, bring to a boil and remove from heat. Toss over cooked noodles. This dish can be served hot or at room temperature. I have found that this sauce recipe easily serves 5 or more. If you are cooking for only 2, don't use all the sauce, instead, put it in a tightly sealed jar. It can keep for weeks, and is a great quick meal.

Playing With Your Food

Guests:
The sauce can be made in advance, then poured on just before people arrive. You can leave this out on the buffet for hours and it still tastes great!

Substitution:
What have I NOT substituted in this recipe?
No chili sauce? Try 1/4 teaspoon hot chili oil, 1/4 teaspoon cayenne, or 1/4 teaspoon Tabasco or equivalent - I've tried them all, they all work
No Szechuan peppercorns? Use red pepper flakes
You can use lime instead of lemon
Use white wine vinegar or more lemon instead of rice vinegar
Once I had no sherry and used white wine. I don't think you can mess this up.

Oops!:
I have accidentally forgotten to sauté the garlic, throwing everything in the pan at once and it was still fine.

S O U P S

Worries go down better with soup than without.
— Jewish Proverb

Stone Soup
European Folk Tale

A stranger arrived in the village one day. He was carrying what looked like his belongings wrapped in a kerchief slung from a stick. My mother peered suspiciously out the window. "Here comes another one of those vagabonds," she muttered. Mother holds no love for vagabonds. She thinks everyone should work hard for a living, or else they're worthless. When we are sitting around by the fire, warming our toes, or staring at the ceiling, she is fit to be tied. "Go out there and get some wood, or at least clean up your bed! You sit around like that, you'll grow up to be nothing but a vagabond!"

Well, of course, I was terribly curious to see one of these vagabonds. I wanted to know about this terrible fate that awaited me. So I dashed out the door towards the square. I heard Mother's voice calling, "Where do you think you're going? You don't just dash out..." but her voice faded away as I ran down the street.

The stranger had carefully removed the kerchief from the stick and was tenderly un-wrapping it. I was afraid, but I kept creeping up closer and closer to see what he had. It was a large stone. He turned, as if he had heard me, and smiled. "See what I have here?" he asked.

"It's a big rock," I answered, puzzled.

"No, no, it's not just a rock," his eyes crinkled up with delight that someone was unable to see what was so obvious to him. "It's magic."

My eyes widened. I stared at it. But nothing happened. No golden aura, no beams of light came shooting out of it. It didn't move, it just sat there... like a stone.

"What does it do?" I asked.

"It makes the most amazing soup."

"No!"

"Yes, absolutely the most delicious, magnificent soup you have ever tasted. But of course, I need a pot." He sat, stroking his chin, musing on where, oh where he might get a pot.

"I can get you a pot!" I exclaimed. Though how I would convince Mother that this stranger needed a pot to make a magic soup was not yet clear.

"You can!" The stranger looked at me delightedly. "Well, you must be a very powerful person in this village."

I puffed up my chest, just a little bit. No one had ever called me powerful before. "I'll be right back."

I ran back into the house. Mother was on her hands and knees, scrubbing the floor. The big soup pot was in its place by the hearth. I couldn't very well sneak the pot out the door. Well, Mother had always said honesty is the best policy.

"Mother, Mother!" I cried. She looked up. "Well that was fast. I thought I lost you for the rest of the day."

"Mother, he's a magician!"

"Oh, is he now."

"Yes, he has a magic stone that makes the most wonderful soup in the world."

"Oh he does, does he. And where is this stone?"

"He has it, in the square! He just needs a pot."

"Hmmm," mused Mother. "I'd like to see that, soup from a stone. A likely story. We'll put an end to this foolishness."

And Mother rose from the floor, grabbed the giant soup pot and together we hauled it to the square.

By now, a few other villagers had gathered. Mother plopped the pot in front of him and with hands on hips said, "All right then, Mr. Magician. Let's see this magic stone."

The Stranger bent down and reverently lifted the stone. He placed it Oh, so carefully into the pot. He looked at it a moment, then looked at the gathered villagers. "The only thing is, I need some water, and a fire."

Well, before you knew it, someone had brought water, wood appeared and soon the pot was on the merrily blazing fire. More villagers were gathering, men on their way home from the fields, women standing in their doorways. We children were everywhere. From his pocket, the Stranger pulled out a spoon and began to carefully stir the soup. After a while, he dipped his spoon and tasted it, smacked his lips. "Mmmmm, this is a good soup. A really good soup. It just needs a little salt."

"I'll get some salt!" the Baker shouted, and lickety split, he arrived with some salt. The Stranger smiled gratefully.

"You are a good man, I promise I'll give you a taste of this soup when it's ready," the Stranger said. The Baker blushed and backed away. The Stranger sprinkled the salt in the pot and tasted it again. "Mmmmm! Lovely." He tasted it again, "But you know, it would be magnificent with a little onion."

The Green Grocer's wife ran into her shop and returned with onions. Once again, the Stranger thanked her graciously and added the onion to the soup. Well, before you know it, the whole village was adding to the soup – carrots, potatoes, spices, The Butcher even insisted on throwing in a couple of chickens. Everyone wanted to be sure they got a taste of the soup.

31

Finally, the Stranger tasted it one more time and announced, "Aha! It's ready! Now I just need a bowl." A bowl appeared and he ladled out some soup. As he ate, we all watched in envy, anticipation, excitement. "Yes, I think it's ready." He nodded as he ate. "I think it's very good. No, I think, in fact that this is the best stone soup I've ever made." He fished around with his spoon and slowly removed his rock, which he carefully wrapped. He looked at us. "Would you like some soup?"

Would we! We went charging up there with bowls and cups, ladles and spoons. Soon the entire village was sitting in the square, smacking our lips at the most delicious soup we had ever tasted.

When the soup was all gone, we looked around. The Stranger was gone. "Huh," said Mother. "Just like a man, disappears when it's time to wash the pot."

Me? When I grow up, I'm going to be a vagabond. I just need to find a magic stone.

Curried Butternut Squash Bisque

6-8 servings

4 tablespoons unsalted butter

2 cups sliced onions

4 - 5 teaspoons curry powder *(Check the taste of your curry. If it's hot, this is too much. Adjust accordingly, and don't believe your jar. If you bought it in an Indian store and it says mild, you may still find it hot.)*

2 medium size butternut squash (about 3 lbs)

2 apples, peeled, cored and coarsely chopped

3 - 4 cups chicken stock

1 cup apple juice

Salt and freshly ground black pepper to taste

1 shredded Granny Smith apple, tossed with a bit of lemon juice or 1 Granny Smith apple, peeled and minced (*optional garnish*)

Yogurt, sour cream or crème fraiche (*optional topping, but great if you used hot curry*)

Melt butter in soup pot. Add onions and curry powder and cook, covered over low heat until onions are tender, 8 - 10 minutes. You want to periodically check and stir them. The lower the heat, the creamier they get. Meanwhile peel the squash (a regular vegetable peeler works best), scrape out the seeds and chop the flesh. Alternatively, you can pre-bake the squash and scrape out the flesh.

When onions are tender, pour in the stock, add squash and the two cored apples. (If you have baked the squash, wait 10 minutes, then add). Bring to a boil, reduce heat and simmer until squash and apples are very tender, about 25 minutes.

Purée solids in food processor with a little of the liquid. Return the purée to the pot, add apple juice. Season to taste with salt and pepper. Thin it to your desired consistency with the reserved liquid. Heat through and serve, either garnished with the shredded or minced apple, or with a dollop of one of the creams on top. Or both!

Playing With Your Food

Guests:

This makes a great first course, but serve small portions because it's very filling.

Substitution:

I have substituted almost everything in this recipe, including the squash! Some things to try: leeks instead of onions, mix up some winter squashes, pears instead of apples. I have left out the apple juice, instead adding an extra apple. Or just skipped the apple altogether, using water or stock to thin it at the end. I've also used cranberry juice, orange juice and even apple sauce in a pinch.

Oops!:
The only thing you don't want to skip is sautéing the onions. This is the key element to any good soup, so just get in the habit. If you find the onions cooked too quickly, it still turns out fine.

Sorrel Soup
(Adapted from the *Silver Palate Cookbook*)
Serves 6 -8

OK. I love this soup. You can eat it cold or hot. It's a totally impractical recipe to include in a book because the main ingredient is... sorrel leaves. Lots of them. They're hard to find, unless you grow it. I have a sorrel plant just so I can have a bowl of this soup once a year. They are only available seasonally at the market, if at all. But if you get your hands on some – yum.

Sorrel is an interesting plant. It's high in oxalic acid, where that tang comes from, so you can't eat a lot of it raw. Oxalic acid can be found in spinach in small amounts, and in rhubarb leaves in toxic amounts. Cooking reduces the acid. You don't have to worry about eating too much sorrel because by the time you've made this soup, you've either used up your whole plant or paid a fortune for that many leaves. Either way, it's a rare treat.

1 stick of butter
2 large yellow onions, peeled and thinly sliced
4 garlic cloves, peeled and chopped.
10 cups tightly packed fresh sorrel leaves, washed and stems removed.
4 cups chicken stock
3/4 cup chopped Italian parsley
1 teaspoon salt

1 teaspoon freshly ground pepper

2 teaspoons ground nutmeg

Pinch of cayenne pepper

1 cup sour cream or yogurt

Snipped fresh chives (garnish)

Melt butter in soup pot. Add onions and garlic and cook, covered over medium heat until tender and lightly colored, about 15 minutes.

Add the sorrel, cover, and cook until it is completely wilted, about 5 minutes. Add stock, parsley, salt, pepper, nutmeg and cayenne, and bring to a boil. Reduce heat, cover and simmer for 50 minutes.

Transfer soup to food processor and purée till smooth. Occasionally, some tough strings from the sorrel turn up after you've puréed. If you want to avoid this, pour the soup through a strainer back into your soup pot. If serving hot, reheat and adjust seasonings to taste. If serving cold, pour into bowl and chill for at least 4 hours, then adjust seasonings. You can put the sour cream or yogurt as a dollop on top, or gently swirl it into the soup to create a beautiful green and white pattern. Garnish with chives.

Playing With Your Food

Guests:

This will impress anyone. It's shockingly good.

Substitution:

Sorrel soup is… sorrel soup. If you don't have any, don't bother.

Oops!:

Same as for all the other soups. Sauté the onions and the rest will be fine.

Zen and the Art of Slicing and Dicing

We generally associate the tea ceremony in Asian traditions with the study of attention. Each aspect of preparing, serving and pouring the tea becomes a practice, a way to follow one's awareness. Engaging in a life activity while practicing mindfulness makes the task a moving meditation.

It's often difficult to remember in the frenzy of meal preparation that a self-awareness practice is possible. The quality of your attention also impacts the quality of a meal – from the thinness of the slices to the consistency of the chopping, to the comfort of your hand and arm as you work.

Many times, professional and amateur cooks experience soreness from chopping. The hand gets fatigued or the arm gets strained. Every finger connects via the muscular-skeletal system up into the shoulder and finally into the ribs and the back. Focusing too intently on one's fine chopping movement without awareness of the rest of yourself creates tension all the way to the back. Conversely, learning to listen to other parts, and enlist bigger muscles can help you to chop more easily, and eventually, more quickly without strain.

Developing awareness of the back and shoulders while chopping can be a pleasurable experience that can enhance your awareness practice as well as improving your slicing and dicing technique. Before you begin a chopping or slicing project, try the following simple series of movements.

Bend your chopping arm at the elbow so that your forearm and hand are vertical, your fingers pointing to the ceiling and your palm in profile. Support your elbow by bringing your other hand across your chest and resting your elbow in or on your opposite hand. Very slowly allow the fingers or your chopping hand to begin drooping down till your hand is limp at the wrist. Just as slowly, uncurl your fingers and straighten your hand so your fingertips reach for the ceiling. Repeat this motion, very slowly, as if you were doing it underwater, several times. Imagine that your fingers are dipping into warm oil that slows them down. If you go slowly enough, you'll notice that some fingers move more easily than others. Do the fingers stay apart or stick together? Notice if any tensions appear: in the shoulders, the forearm, the neck, even your face. Sometimes we chop just as hard with the jaw as with the knife! After doing this movement about 10 times, let your arms come down and just pause. Feel the difference in your two hands.

Now extend your working arm straight out in front of you. Begin lengthening your arm, as if someone was pulling it forward, or as if you were reaching for something, then let it return. As you do this movement, what do you feel in your shoulder blade? In your upper arm? Many times we just reach with the arm, never engaging the big muscles in the back. Can you let your shoulder blade move? Sense the movement in your ribs as your shoulder blade slides along them. After about 10 times, let your arm come down. Notice if you feel anything different in your two arms.

Now raise this same arm straight up to the ceiling. How did you do that? Was it painful? Difficult? If you fold your arm so your hand moves toward your face first, then let the hand travel upward, it can be much easier for people with shoulder problems. However, if even that hurts, you can do this same movement with your arm extended in front like before. Imagine that you have a light bulb in your hand. Begin a turning movement with your hand and arm as if you were screwing the light bulb in, then unscrewing, turning your hand and your whole arm first one direction, then the other. Can you turn your arm in such a way that you can feel your shoulder blade move? Once again, after about 10 moves, slowly lower your arm.

Of course at this point, your other arm might be jealous! If you wish to do the same thing with your non-chopping arm, feel free. Otherwise, pick up your knife and see if chopping feels a little different now.

Chicken Soup

4 servings

Some people would call this the world's most important dish. Chicken soup can also be the easiest. Instead of the stone in the story told above, just think chicken. It is the secret ingredient, and has proven to cure many a "common cold". Certain people may be born knowing how to make chicken soup, but I have been asked many times for this recipe, so if you aren't of Eastern European peasant stock, or even if you are, but you skipped this lesson on your mother's knee, this recipe is for you.

2 tablespoons butter or olive oil

2 medium sized onions - chopped

2 - 4 cloves garlic - minced (if you have a cold, use a lot)

1 chicken - cut up

1/4 cup white wine

2 carrots - sliced. If they are fat, halve the slices

2 sticks celery - diced

1 1/2 quarts water

1 - 2 bay leaves

1/2 teaspoon freshly ground pepper

Salt and pepper to taste

1/2 teaspoon dried thyme

1 teaspoon dried marjoram

1/2 teaspoon dried sage

2 potatoes - diced - if they are organic, don't bother peeling them

In a soup pot, heat butter or olive oil over medium heat. Add onions and sauté till they get a little soft. Add the garlic and the chicken. Brown the chicken pieces on all sides. This can be tricky with the onions, make sure the onions don't burn on the bottom of the pan. If you are timid, you can remove the onions, add the chicken, then put the onions back in. Pour in the wine and quickly deglaze (see note) the pot. Add the water, carrots, celery and spices. Cook for around 25 minutes, then add the potatoes. Cook another 20 minutes, adjust seasonings and serve. This soup is even better the next day.

There are folks who think serving chicken soup with the bones is messy and gauche. It's funny that Americans are perfectly fine with eating barbecued chicken with their hands, but the idea of grabbing a bone out of their soup is considered indelicate. There are other cultures that relish the bone. They break the bone, sucking the vital marrow, making a delightful mess. Somewhere in between is leaving the chicken on the bone and providing a bowl on the table for discarded bones, broken and whole. If you or your guests are of the more delicate variety, allow the soup to cool enough that you can scoop the chicken out with a slotted spoon and remove the meat from the bones. It should just fall off. Re-heat the soup. The only danger with this process is that inevitably, a small bone escapes back into the soup.

Note: Deglazing is a fancy word for getting rid of the brown crust on the bottom of the pan. Keeping the pan hot, quickly pour in the wine, have a wooden spoon handy. The minute the wine hits the pan, there's a sizzle. Use your spoon to quickly scrape the crust, before all the wine evaporates. It's really exciting and adds an awesome flavor to the soup.

Playing With Your Food

Substitution:

This basic recipe can be adapted in countless ways.

a) Use noodles or rice instead of potatoes (add in the last 10 minutes, or just add cooked noodles at the end).

b) You can use beef and it becomes a beef vegetable soup.

c) You can skip the meat altogether and just triple all the veggies, adding your favorite meat substitute (chicken flavored seitan* also works well)

d) Missing an herb? Leave it out. Got some fresh parsley in the house? Throw it in! If you have fresh herbs for any of the above, a general rule of thumb is that you triple the amount of fresh to dried.

e) And if you don't want to use wine, you can deglaze with water.

Oops:

Sometimes, you're just too sick for the fancy stuff. Cut everything up and just throw it all in the pot. It will still heal you.

Main Courses

If you can get nothing better out of the world, get a good dinner

out of it, at least.

— Herman Melville

What's for Dinner?

When my mother was a young girl, she lived on a farm with her extended family. One day, her sister-in-law saw one of the geese staggering down the path. It fell down at her feet. Thinking it had died, and these being hard times, my aunt decided the goose would be dinner. She sat down and plucked the goose, then went inside to get a pot. Meanwhile the goose, who had actually gotten stinking drunk eating fermented blackberries, regained consciousness. When my aunt returned with the pot, the naked goose was staggering back to the blackberry bushes for more.

I've always been touched by this story, perhaps because I sometimes feel like that goose. How often I've wandered down the garden path of life, getting myself into regrettable situations. Then somehow, after the damage was done, I went right back and made the same stupid mistakes all over again. Many times someone has even turned to me and said, "Well, my dear, this time your goose is cooked," whatever that means.

Usually we end up repeating ourselves because we are propelled by compulsion into making the same choices. "What am I doing? Where am I going? Why did I do that? What was I thinking?" can leave me staggering from option to option till I end up back at the blackberries.

If only life choices were as simple as answering the question, "What's for dinner?" Although for some, even that is overwhelming. Many times, I'll come home from a week of teaching out of town, open my fridge and find that all the food I left there for my husband Ron is still sitting there, albeit slightly moldy. I'll ask him what he ate for dinner all week. "Pizza and peanut butter."

"Why didn't you eat anything else?"

"There was nothing in the fridge."

From a bewilderment of options to an inability to see the options around us, our perceived limitations take the intentionality out of our actions. Whether one is paralyzed by too many options, or can only see the peanut butter, one is limited.

While the following main courses may answer the question, "What's for dinner?" the other exciting possibility is exploring "How will I make it?" Is it possible to prepare a main course in a relaxed fashion, without fear of failure, without rushing, without excess tension?

Here is an exercise to try as you make dinner. The nice thing about it is that you don't have to stop your preparations at all. It involves your breath. There are dozens of schools of breathing techniques these days. I love what Moshe Feldenkrais once said about breathing techniques. "Telling people they should breathe this way or that way, is like telling a man that in order to win a girl, he must always wear this suit, put this rose in his lapel, he must always say the same words. We know that doesn't work. Well breathing is the same. Different situations require different kinds of breathing."

Exploring the options available in your breath can perhaps offer new options for the way you prepare the meal, or even how you live your life.

Begin by noticing your breath. For a few breaths, just listen. Don't try to fix anything or change it. Notice what moves as you breathe. Do you feel movement in your belly? Your chest? Your back? Your shoulders? It doesn't matter if you do or don't, but just notice.

Intentionally, inhibit the movement of the breath in your belly. For three to four breaths, continue, but don't let your belly move. Then let that go and breathe normally. What does your breath feel like now? Try the same thing again, this time holding the chest still. Notice how freezing your chest affects the quality of the movement of the breath. Then notice what happens when you let that go. You can do this with your back and/or your shoulders as well, or just do one part. Each time you try it, you may have a different experience. And you may discover that your cooking experience is different as well.

I haven't yet perfected cooking a real goose, but hopefully some of these main courses will not leave *you* staggering by dinner time.

Roasted Chicken with Rosemary and Garlic
Serves 4 – 6

1 3 – 4 lb. chicken
4 – 5 sprigs fresh rosemary
4 – 5 cloves peeled garlic – average size, if they are really big, split them
Salt & pepper
1 tablespoon Dijon mustard
2 tablespoons olive oil

Preheat oven to 425 degrees. Meanwhile, prepare the chicken. You are going to insert the rosemary and garlic between the skin and the flesh of the bird. This may sound like a creepy or outrageous idea, but it's actually no big deal. You start by the cavity and gently pull the skin away a little at a time. You don't have to separate the whole thing. Insert the rosemary sprigs and garlic under the skin, pushing them in and distributing as best you can through the breast and down to the leg joint area. Try not to prick the skin with the rosemary stem. Put one sprig of rosemary in the cavity.

Rub the entire chicken with the Dijon mustard, then salt and pepper it. Drizzle the olive oil on top. Place in the oven and immediately turn the temperature down to 350 degrees. Bake 1 - 1 1/2 hours depending on its size. After about a half hour, you will start having juices that you can use for basting, at which point, baste every 10 - 15 minutes. Officially, the internal temperature of the chicken should be between 160 - 170 degrees. But if you don't have a thermometer, you can still easily test for doneness. The skin will be a nice brown. The juice runs a clear yellow with no blood if you stick a fork in the leg joint. If you're really nervous, take it out and cut it at the joint of the leg. If the flesh is slightly pink, it's OK, but if it's bloody or red, put it back in for a few minutes.

Let the chicken rest for about 10 minutes after removing from oven. Save the juices to pour on the chicken, or make into a gravy.

Playing With Your Food

Guests:
People love roast chicken. One chicken will easily serve 4 people, but if you are planning a dinner party, you may want to do two. Two chickens in the oven will affect your cooking time. It's an ideal thing to cook if you want to hang out and have appetizers for a while without having to monitor the progress of the main course.

Substitution:

You can make this as simple as you want, you can even roast a chicken with nothing but salt and pepper. Or try using sage leaves instead of rosemary.

Oops!:

If you forget to preheat the oven, the chicken will still cook, it will just take a little longer and the skin won't be as crispy at the end.

If you do prick through the skin with your rosemary, no harm done, just some juice will escape.

Fire:

I once put a chicken in the oven, then forgot to turn the heat down to 350. To make matters worse, I forgot the chicken was in the oven, went to teach a class, and remembered when I was going home, almost 2 hours later. Believe it or not, the chicken was still delicious – a little crispy, but definitely edible. So you're unlikely to burn down the house!

Party Chicken
(adapted from the Silver Palate Cookbook)
Serves about 15

This recipe is for party size. When I do it for just one chicken, I halve the marinade ingredients, it seems to work better than dividing by 4, maybe because most chickens are bigger than 2 1/2 lb. Also, you can chop the chicken into smaller pieces – wings separate, legs and thighs separate. It works much better as party food that way. This is one of the easiest and most delicious chicken recipes I've ever tasted. But you do have to remember to start the marinade the day before!

    4 chickens, 2 1/2 lbs. each, quartered

    1 head of garlic, peeled and puréed

    1/4 cup dried oregano

Salt and freshly ground pepper to taste

1/2 cup red wine vinegar

1/2 cup olive oil

1 cup pitted prunes

1/2 cup pitted Spanish green olives

1/2 cup capers with a bit of juice

6 bay leaves

1 cup brown sugar

1 cup white wine

1/4 cup parsley or cilantro, finely chopped

In a large bowl combine chicken, garlic, oregano, pepper and salt, vinegar, olive oil, prunes, olives, capers and juice, and bay leaves. Cover and let marinate, refrigerated, overnight. If you can, periodically toss the chicken around in the marinade.

Preheat oven to 350 degrees.

Arrange chicken in a single layer in one or two large, shallow baking pans and spoon marinade over it evenly. Sprinkle chicken pieces with brown sugar and pour white wine around them.

Bake for 50 minutes to 1 hour, basting frequently with pan juices. Chicken is done when thigh pieces, pricked with a fork at their thickest, yield clear yellow (rather than pink) juice.

With a slotted spoon transfer chicken, prunes, olives and capers to a serving platter. Moisten with a few spoonfuls of pan juices and sprinkle generously with parsley or cilantro. Pass remaining pan juices in a sauceboat.

To serve cold, cool to room temperature in cooking juices before transferring to a serving platter. If chicken has been covered and refrigerated, allow it to return to a room temperature before serving. Spoon some of the reserved juice over chicken.

Playing With Your Food

Substitution:
If you are out of white wine, use red wine. It's a slightly different flavor, but still great.
Once we cooked this recipe for a Frenchman who hated garlic, using shallots instead.
Deelish. It's also not super important that the vinegar be red wine vinegar. Innovate!

Oops!:
Once, in a moment of complete inattention, I mixed the brown sugar and the wine into
the marinade and didn't even realize it till the next day when I was about to put the
chicken in the oven. It was not as rich tasting, the wine had obviously diluted the
power of the marinade, but no one noticed except me. I don't recommend it, but it's just
about the only thing you can do wrong, and it's still not a disaster.

Wrapped and Stuffed Portabella Mushrooms
Serves 2

This recipe is a testimony to the fact that you can get away with just about any
substitution or innovation. Years ago, I cut out a recipe for pastry wrapped portabella mushrooms. I made the dish once or twice, then lost the recipe. Over the
years, I tried to reconstruct it for myself. One day, as I was perusing one of my
cookbooks, the recipe fell out! I stared at it unbelievingly. It had almost nothing to
do with the version I had developed over the years. Following are both versions;
you'll see I really went pretty far from the original. Hopefully you'll enjoy both
takes on a truly delicious way to prepare portabellas!

Lavinia's version:
The easy way to do this is to use puff pastry dough - one sheet for each mushroom. A more challenging and crispy way is to use phyllo dough, which makes the
meal lighter, but more work.

2 portabella mushrooms, stems removed

2 sheets defrosted puff pastry or 8 - 16 sheets defrosted phyllo dough*

(if using phyllo, ¼ - ½ cup melted butter)

1 tablespoon olive oil

1/2 medium onion, coarsely chopped

1 clove garlic

6 sundried tomatoes, rehydrated

1/4 cup walnuts or pine nuts

1/4 cup crumbled feta or soft-style goat cheese

1/4 cup basil or parsley leaves, or a combination of both

1 teaspoon dried oregano

1/4 cup bread crumbs

Salt and pepper to taste

Preheat oven to 350 degrees. Sauté onions and garlic over low heat till turning golden. Add tomatoes and immediately remove from heat. Put all the ingredients except the mushrooms and pastry in a food processor, process till blended. With the mushrooms upside down, spread mixture across the gills. Place gill side down on pastry dough. Bring up the corners to meet, seal them together, then place the mushrooms on a baking sheet with the top side down, so that the pastry folds are on the pan.

If you are using phyllo, spread one sheet out. Baste the sheet with melted butter, then place another sheet on top. You can do this for 4 - 8 layers, depending on how crusty you like it. I use about 5. When working with phyllo, make sure the minute you unroll it from the package, you cover it with a damp cloth. Keep the unused phyllo covered with the damp cloth: for each layer, remove the cloth, take out one sheet at a time and immediately replace the cloth. Once you have your layers, place your mushroom in the center, gill side down, and fold the sheets around the top. Place folded side down on baking sheet.

Bake in oven till brown, about 30 - 40 minutes.

The Original (mostly)
Portabella Mushroom with Mushroom–Pecan Paté
2 portobello mushrooms, stems removed
1 - 2 sheets defrosted puff pastry or 8 - 16 sheets defrosted phyllo dough
(if using phyllo, 1/4 - 1/2 cup melted butter)

Paté:
10 - 14 white (button) mushrooms
2 cloves garlic, peeled
1 green onion, trimmed
1/4 cup toasted pecans
Olive oil as needed
Salt and pepper to taste

Optional Topping:
2 oz. Chopped crimini, wild or white mushrooms
1 to 2 green onions, finely sliced
1 - 2 teaspoons olive oil or butter

Preheat oven to 375 degrees. Clean and remove stems from portobellos. Wipe off button mushrooms (see note). In a food processor, finely chop button mushrooms, garlic, green onions and pecans. Drizzle in small amount of oil to make a paste.

Depending on the size of the mushroom, and your caloric preferences, you can either use one piece of puff pastry per mushroom, or take one piece, place it on a large piece of wax paper and GENTLY roll it out to stretch it for both. Puff pastry is very rich, which is why it tastes so good. But you can reduce the caloric content with the stretch approach. Cut it to shape around the mushroom.

Divide the mushroom–pecan mixture and spread the paté on the pastry, covering most of it – center outwards. Place the Portobello gill side up. Wrap the dough around the mushroom, closing flaps and trimming pastry if necessary. Place mushrooms gill side down on a cookie sheet. Bake 20 minutes, or until golden brown.

If using phyllo, follow instructions for layering from above recipe. Then spread the paté and wrap as above.

While mushrooms are baking, chop the mushrooms for the topping. Sauté the mushrooms and green onions in butter or oil till just tender. Top the baked pastry with this when serving.

Playing With Your Food

Guests:
I've served this to vegetarian and non-vegetarian friends alike and everyone has loved it.

Substitution:
As you can see, substitution can create a whole new dish. Feel free to play with mixtures that you like with mushrooms. Use shallots instead of onions. Bacon and blue cheese. The possibilities are deliciously endless.

Forgot the dough? you can also just use pie dough (see recipe on pg. ___) instead of puff pastry.

Oops!:
As you may have noticed, in my version I put the paste on the gills, in the original on the dough. So I guess this recipe really is foolproof.

Chicken with Tarragon Mayonnaise
Serves 6

Great for parties, picnics. The mayonnaise is awesome on potato salad as well.

3 12 - 14 oz. chicken breasts (with bone)

2 extra large egg yolks

2 tablespoons tarragon vinegar

2 - 3 tablespoons chopped tarragon leaves

2 teaspoons Madagascar green peppercorns packed in brine, drained

3 - 4 sprigs parsley

1 teaspoon salt

1/4 teaspoon freshly ground pepper

1 cup oil - soy, peanut, olive or blend

2 tablespoons heavy cream (optional)

1 tablespoon finely chopped shallots

Bake the chicken breasts at 375 degrees for 30-45 minutes. Cool to room temperature. Carefully remove all the meat from the bones, discarding the skin, fat, and tendons. Cut into bite size pieces. Place the chicken in a mixing bowl and set aside.

Tarragon Mayonnaise

In the food processor, place al the ingredients except the oil, heavy cream and shallots. Process to a smooth paste. Keeping the food processor running, pour the oil in a slow stream till it gets thick and shiny. Transfer to a small bowl and stir in the cream if you're using it.

Spoon the tarragon mayonnaise over the chicken. Add the shallots and mix thoroughly. Chill for 15 minutes, adjust the seasoning and serve. Or place the salad in the refrigerator and remove 1 hour before serving.

Fear of Mayonnaise

Every time I make mayonnaise, someone asks in disbelief, "You made it from scratch?" Yet in Europe and Quebec, people make mayonnaise as regularly as an omelet. Somewhere in US cuisine mythology, we have developed fear of failed mayonnaise. Or maybe it's raw egg phobia.

It's true, there may not be such a thing as a foolproof approach. Some recipes insist on room temperature eggs. Some say vinegar, others lemon. I've succeeded and failed at both. I have found the most crucial elements are the acid balance, making sure you have all the ingredients in a nice paste before pouring in the oil and ABSOLUTELY pouring the olive oil in a tiny, steady stream. And only use the egg yolk. If you go too fast, or in spurts, it doesn't work. If your mayonnaise fails, call it chicken salad with a tarragon dressing. A little watery, but still tasty. Or sigh and begin again. Everything improves with practice. However, some processes in the kitchen are still like alchemy and often when I'm making mayonnaise, I feel like the sorcerer's apprentice. I almost hear the music as the liquid thickens and turns into that luscious spread. I have learned that it's not worth trying to "rescue" a failed mayonnaise. Just accept that you wasted an egg and some oil and start again.

If this process is too terrifying, here is the cheater's approach. Take a really good mayonnaise; Hellman's or here in the South, we have Duke's. Chop up all the other ingredients (tarragon, peppercorns, etc.) and stir them into the mayonnaise. It will taste almost the same, without the fear of failure. In fact, I've been told by Europeans that they love our jars of mayonnaise.

Playing With Your Food

Guests:
This is great at a party. You don't have to worry about keeping it warm or cold.

Substitution:
You can use onion instead of shallots, you may need a little more and it's not as "sophisticated" a taste, but it works.
If you can't find tarragon vinegar, just use white wine vinegar.
Living out in the "provinces" it's not easy to find green peppercorns in brine. (You can order them online now!) I've used dried ones that I soaked in some vinegar. I've

skipped that ingredient altogether. It's still OK.

You can use boneless, skinless chicken breast. Not as flavorful, but quick and easy.

Cook them for a shorter time – 25 minutes or so.

Leek Pie (with variations)
Serves 6 - 8

This was known for years by my family as the Tofu Leek Pie. In truth, it had begun as a recipe for Leek Pie from the Joy of Cooking; a recipe that called for a ton of sour cream. While going through a vegan phase, I experimented till I found a way to make tofu not taste like tofu. After a while, I forgot that it had ever had any other ingredients. One day, after I'd already begun sautéing the leeks, I discovered that my tofu had mutated into a bizarre, mold covered science project. Not willing to give up the meal (see the Red Peppers story), I improvised and discovered that leeks will forgive almost any attempt at sabotage – hence Leek Pie with variations.

Two big leeks.

4 tablespoons unsalted butter

1/2 teaspoon salt

12 oz. silken tofu*, or 1 1/2 cup sour cream, or yogurt, or ricotta cheese, or 1 cup of any of those with some grated or crumbled cheese - feta, cheddar, asiago, all work great.

2 tablespoons lemon juice - if you are using tofu

1 egg, beaten

1 tablespoon chopped fresh dill or 1 teaspoon dried

Salt and pepper

1 cooked slice of bacon, crumbled for topping (optional)

Crust:

1 cup unbleached white, whole wheat pastry (see note) or a combo of both flours

Pinch of salt

1 stick unsalted butter, cut into small pieces

3 tablespoons cold (iced) water

Note on flour: If you are new to whole wheat flour, you should know that there are two kinds: bread flour and pastry flour. While you can make bread flour into a crust, it is difficult. Whole wheat *pastry* flour will cooperate more for your pie crusts. Adding a tablespoon of cornstarch per cup of flour will help hold your crust together. You can also mix half whole wheat and half white. That being said, if you want the smooth traditional look of a crust, don't even bother with whole wheat.

Preheat the oven to 425 degrees.

Crust:

Put flour and salt into food processor. Pulse a few seconds. Add butter, pulse several times till it's mixed in and has texture of corn meal. Add water a little at a time, till absorbed. Roll it out gently, do not overwork it, and press it into a pie pan. When rolling out your dough, one huge time and frustration saver is to roll it out between two pieces of wax paper. Just make sure you put flour both on bottom sheet and on top of the crust before you place the top sheet. It is almost 100% hassle free. You can finish the edging in two ways: 1) Pinch a bit of dough between thumb and forefinger, then move down past the width of that finger and pinch again, going all around the pie pan, or 2) Press down with the tines of a fork all around the edge. Trim excess dough.

Note: Some people think the only good crust is made by hand. I have found that many times, people overwork their crusts. By using the food processor, you save time and don't make the crust too tough. Of course, if you don't have one, you can still do it by hand, just don't over knead. Many recipes tell you to use two knives to make the pastry. I just use my fingers – it's faster and better and you get to squish the dough around. Cut the butter into small chunks first. Then work the butter into the flour until the dough looks like coarse cornmeal. It really does happen!

Filling:

Clean the leeks by splitting lengthwise, taking them to the sink and washing each layer to remove all sand. The upper white part on the outer leaves is especially dirty. Slice thinly. You can use the green part about ¾ of the way up, unless your leaves are old and brown. Remove any tough or old looking leaves as you slice. Melt butter in saucepan, add leeks and 1/2 teaspoon salt, and cook slowly till they are nice and soft. It should take 10 - 15 minutes. Remove from heat and let cool.

If you are using tofu, put it in the food processor with the lemon juice, and some salt and pepper to taste. Then mix all the ingredients except the bacon in a bowl, make sure the leeks are not so hot they start cooking the egg. Blend it well, add salt and pepper to taste. Sprinkle the crumbled bacon on top if you are using it. Place in the oven. Let it bake for 10 minutes at 425 degrees, then reduce the heat to 350 degrees and bake for another 40 minutes or so. Each oven is different. The top should be light brown, the crust golden brown. The center should not be jiggly – its firmness is somewhat dependent on whether you used tofu or dairy, so rely on the color. It will set up more as it cools. Remove and let it set at least 15 minutes.

Playing With Your Food

Substitution:
This pie is like a quiche, you can put almost anything in it if you add egg.
If you don't have enough leeks, use onions.
You can also garnish the top of this with pieces of sausage.

Oops!:
I've forgotten to put the salt in the crust and added it as I was rolling the dough, put the water in with the butter, it's all OK!

Barbados Black Bean Cakes With Mango Salsa

4 generous servings

Mango Salsa:

2 cups peeled, diced mango

1/2 cup diced red bell pepper

1/4 cup finely diced red onion

1 Serrano pepper

2 tablespoons coarsely chopped cilantro

2 teaspoons peeled, minced fresh ginger root (see note on peeling ginger pg. 16)

1/4 teaspoon salt

1 tablespoon lime juice

Black Bean Cakes:

2 15 oz. cans black beans, drained and rinsed, or if you cook from scratch, about 1 3/4 cups cooked beans.

1/4 cup chopped cilantro or parsley

1/4 cup chopped red onion

1 egg, slightly beaten

1 teaspoon ground cumin

1 teaspoon minced garlic

1/2 teaspoon ground allspice

1/2 teaspoon salt

1/8 teaspoon cayenne

1/3 cup bread crumbs

1 tablespoon olive oil

Chopped cilantro and lime wedges for garnish (optional)

Salsa:

Combine all salsa ingredients in a bowl. Set aside.

Make sure that you drained the beans very well. If there is too much moisture, it makes the patties difficult to work with. Place beans in a large bowl and coarsely mash until they stick together. Add cilantro or parsley, onion, egg, cumin, garlic, allspice, salt and cayenne. Mix until well blended. Divide mixture into 8 equal parts. Shape into 1/2 inch thick patties.

Coat patties with bread crumbs. They can be delicate and crumbly, so you might want to put the patties on wax paper so you can transfer easily to the frying pan.

Heat oil in a skillet over medium heat. Add bean cakes and fry until golden brown on both sides, turning once, about 8 minutes total. Serve with salsa and garnishes.

Playing With Your Food

Guests:
Check if they like cilantro – it's a love it or hate it kind of herb.

Substitution:
Cilantro can be skipped if you realize you don't have it.
If Serrano peppers are hard to find, use jalapeños or some other chile peppers – just check the heat on them and adjust the amount accordingly. Don't have red onions? Use what's on hand.
I once lost this recipe and added oranges to the salsa because I thought I remembered that as an ingredient. I had guests over and they kept asking for the recipe.

Fire:
Just keep your eye on the patties – they can brown quickly.

Zucchini Kofta Balls with Fragrant Tomato Gravy

(Adapted from *Lord Krishna's Cuisine*)

Serves 4

This amazing dish is a requirement during summer when you are drowning in tomatoes and are leaving zucchinis in strangers' cars. It sounds labor intensive, but if you just follow the instructions, it can't fail.

Gravy:

15 - 17 plum tomatoes or 4-5 large regular tomatoes (about 2 lbs)

3 tablespoons blanched almonds or raw cashews

1/4 teaspoon fennel seeds

1 teaspoon cumin seeds

1 - 2 hot green chiles, seeded and broken into bits

1/2 inch piece of peeled fresh ginger root, sliced (see note on peeling ginger pg. 16)

1/2 tablespoon jaggery* or brown sugar

1/2 teaspoon turmeric

1 tablespoon tomato paste

4 tablespoons ghee* or olive oil

3 tablespoons chopped fresh cilantro or parsley

1/2 cup vegetable stock or water

1 teaspoon salt

How to peel tomatoes. You have two options – 1) Fill a pot with water and bring to boil. Cut a cross on the bottom of each tomato. Drop the tomatoes into the boiling water and count to 15, or until you start to see flaps of skin where you cut the cross (some tomatoes are quicker, others take longer. Remove the tomatoes and plunge them into a bowl of ice water. The peel should come right off. They will be watery so chop in a bowl to catch the juice. 2) Freeze the tomatoes, then pop them in the microwave for 30 seconds to 1 minute. The skin comes right off. I just

58

keep tomatoes in my freezer so I have them on hand. After you have peeled them, squeeze the tomato over a strainer in a bowl. The strainer catches the seeds, the juice goes in the bowl, which you will add to your sauce.

After you have peeled and squeezed the tomatoes, dice the tomatoes and put aside.

Place the nuts, fennel seeds and cumin seeds into the food processor. Pulse on and off until coarsely powdered. Add the reserved tomato juice, green chiles, ginger, sweetener, turmeric, tomato paste and enough water to yield 2/3 cup of liquid. (I have found that I usually don't have to add any water.) Process until smooth.

Heat the ghee or oil over moderate heat in a big saucepan. When it is warm, carefully add the tomato liquid. Stir it up, partially cover and cook for a few minutes – a tomato purée separates from the oil. Stir in the diced tomatoes, half of the fresh herbs and the stock or water. (While stock is nice, this sauce is really just as good with water.) Reduce the heat to low and simmer, partially covered, for about 30 minutes. Stir it occasionally to help the tomatoes break down. It will look like a nice gravy or tomato sauce. Add the salt and the remaining fresh herbs. This sauce can keep for several days if you have leftovers.

As the sauce is simmering, you can prepare the kofta balls:

3 cups coarsely shredded seedless summer squash: zucchini, patty pan, crookneck, yellow squash. All work well (about 1 lb.)

1-2 hot green chilies, seeded and minced

1/2 inch piece of scraped, minced fresh ginger root.

3 tablespoons finely chopped cilantro or parsley

1 teaspoon salt

1/2 teaspoon baking powder

Vegetable oil (peanut oil is great for this) for deep frying

About 1 cup of chick pea flour* (sifted before measuring)

One of the easiest ways to shred squash is to use the grating attachment of your food processor. But even grating by hand is pretty fast. Take your grated squash to the sink. Grab a handful at a time and squeeze as much water as you can from the squash. Place the dry squash in a separate bowl. (if you put it back in the same bowl, it re-absorbs water.) Add the green chilies, ginger, fresh herbs, salt and baking powder and blend together.

If your gravy is done, you can begin to make the koftas. Pour about 2 1/2 - 3 inches of oil into a deep frying pan or wok over moderately high heat. While the oil is heating (it takes about 5 - 7 minutes), pour the flour into the squash mixture. Knead by hand until ingredients are just blended. Have a plate or wax paper handy. Quickly form about 20 balls. The longer it takes, the more water from the squash loosens the mixture. When the balls are ready, raise the heat on your oil. If you are into kitchen science, the ideal temperature is 355 degrees. You can test your oil by just dropping a little bit of the mixture into the pan. It should instantly start to sizzle and bubble. If the oil is too cool, your balls will absorb too much oil. If it's too hot, you'll notice right away that the koftas are browning too quickly. I prefer making slightly smaller balls and cooking on a higher heat, it makes for a lighter ball. But this is a fun place to experiment with the joys of frying.

When the balls are a golden brown, remove with a slotted spoon and drain on paper towels. You can keep them warm in a 250 degree oven. Let the oil re-heat before the next batch.

You can serve them two ways: the balls on a plate and pass the gravy, so that people can choose their mixture. This keeps the balls a little crunchy. Or you can put the balls into the sauce, and then they absorb the flavor.

Playing With Your Food

Guests:
While this is a bit time-consuming to make, it is a great dish when you have vegetarians and non-vegetarians, because everyone loves it.

Substitutions:
I recently started making these, then realized I was out of fresh ginger and chilies. I used a pinch of cayenne and skipped the ginger. They were still delicious.

Oops:
The messiest part is making the balls. Don't worry if they don't exactly look round – they even out in the cooking. Make sure you have a towel on hand to wipe your hands!

Fire:
These seem to cook slowly, and suddenly, they're done. Be careful not to walk away in the last couple of minutes.

Pad Thai

Serves 4

This is an amalgamation of many recipes I've tried through the years. You can vary the protein based on your taste (and diet of the moment.) I find it highly irritating that this simple dish is sold in a box at the health food Store for over $4, since it costs pennies to make. Of course the Asian stores now carry something called Pad Thai sauce which is great in a pinch, but I'm a big fan of fresh.

8 -10 oz. Pad Thai noodles (fat rice noodles)

4 tablespoons distilled white vinegar or rice vinegar

3 tablespoons tomato paste

3 tablespoons water

2 tablespoons sugar

1 -2 tablespoons vegetable oil

2 cloves minced garlic

1 fresh green chile, seeded and minced

2 teaspoons tamarind juice* (optional)

2 eggs

Fish Sauce – to taste – these come in different strengths of saltiness and fishiness. I'd start with a teaspoon and add while cooking. (optional)

Salt to taste – do the fish sauce first if you're using it

1/4 cup chopped cilantro (optional)

1 cup bean sprouts

1 cup chopped, unsalted, roasted peanuts (optional)

Lime (or lemon) wedges

Chopped or sliced green onion (scallion)

8 oz. Protein: cooked, diced chicken or pork, shrimp, tofu, even cooked pieces of salmon can work

Noodles:

Pad Thai noodles are tricky. You don't boil them, you put them in boiling water. Many of them have instructions to leave them in there for 10 minutes. But I have found that often, in 10 minutes you can have a sticky, glutinous mass of goo. I suggest you put them in the hot water and test them every two minutes. As soon as they feel ready, get them out of the water and plunge them into cold water, making sure they are separate. They will be hot again when you sauté them with the sauce.Sauce:

In a bowl, mix together vinegar, tomato paste, water and sugar. Set aside. In a frying pan, heat oil and stir-fry garlic and chili on medium heat for 3 minutes. Add your protein and sauté another 2 minutes. Stir in tomato-vinegar mixture. Add fish sauce, tamarind juice and salt. Make a well in the center of the pan, crack in eggs and cook until almost set, about 2 minutes, then stir quickly into sauce. Let sauce mixture continue to simmer on low heat until very thick, about 4 – 5 minutes. Toss noodles into sauce, making sure it is heated through. Add the green onion. Serve with lime wedges, peanuts and bean sprouts on side of plate. If desired, garnish with cilantro.

Playing With Your Food

Substitutions:
You can really mix anything into this noodle combo. If you have no bean sprouts, use shredded carrots or sautéed cabbage.
No cilantro? Use parsley.
Even if you don't have fish sauce or tamarind juice (not in everyone's cupboard), you can still have a tasty dish, just add lemon to the stir fry and a bit more salt.
And if you are vegan, just skip the eggs.

Oops:
I must confess I have thrown the noodles into the water, then forgotten about them. The best rescue is to immediately throw them into ice water. Better though is to have a little timer to remind you.

Cooking with Love (or with your Love)

Cooking is like love. It should be entered into with abandon or not at all.
—Harriet Van Horne

I've embarrassed my husband Ron more than once at restaurants. While I generally refuse to even walk into a fast food establishment, when circumstances (like Ron longing for a burger) demand it, I accept that the substance they call food is just processed industrial waste and that the workers there have no relationship whatsoever with the coated, packaged corn by-products they call chicken nuggets or Whoppers. However, when we go to a restaurant where waiters scurry about murmuring things like "The gnocchi are light, prepared with fresh chanterelles and the first corn of the season, delightfully sweet soupçons of flavor in a delicate marsala sauce," I expect love to emanate from the food. And when the waiter has the audacity to approach our table with some formulaic question like, "Is everything delicious?" or "Are we pleased?" my husband cringes if the meal has not registered on my love meter.

"No, we are not pleased," I will answer calmly. "Or maybe you're pleased, since I don't know who you mean by we, but this meal was clearly not prepared with love." By this time, Ron will either have excused himself from the table for a sudden run to the men's room, or is busily cutting a pea into microscopic pieces on his plate. I know it's a hopeless cause. I know the waiter goes back into the kitchen, rolls her eyes and tells the chef there's a nut out there complaining that her food was made without love. They both snort in derision and toss the offending entrée into the trash. It doesn't matter. Like Don Quixote and his impossible dream, I imagine a world where love is an essential ingredient of the meal.

In *Like Water for Chocolate*, a wonderful film about a woman who loved cooking, an unpleasant relative rhapsodizes over a particular dish at a party. "What is in this? It's sublime!"

"Oh, peppers, garlic, cumin, some cinnamon and... love," the heroine replies.

I am not alone.

So one would think that cooking a meal together with one's love would double the love quotient in the meal, right? After all, harmony and joy abound when surrounded by fresh basil, Yukon gold potatoes, a gorgeous piece of wild salmon. It can only be compounded by the presence of the significant other.

"So, what can I do to help?" he asks, casting an unmistakable look of derision at my apron which is covered in tomato seeds and batter, the floor crusted with zucchini gratings, the counters spilling with dirty food processor, four knives coated with various unidentifiable substances and several dripping bowls while the oven timer beeps madly. I look around, at first thinking, well, there's nothing he can do. I've got it all under control. I am a control freak after all.

"Well, you can either help me clean some of this stuff up, or you can grate the cheese." He opts for the cheese, which I need in a moment to mix into the gratin. I return to the delicate task of thinly slicing the potatoes. He wanders around for a few minutes, then opens the refrigerator to stare inside. "What ARE you looking for?" My inner timer is needing the cheese.

"The cheese. What kind of cheese are we using?"

"You're joking."

"No, what's the big deal?"

"The cheese and the grater are on the counter, right where you were standing when I asked you to grate it!"

"Well, how did you expect me to see it with all the crap you have all over the counter?"

"I offered you the option of cleaning. If the sight of food preparation is so offensive to you... "

"It's not that. I just can't believe you can work in such chaos."

"Me? Me work in chaos? Have you looked in your studio lately?"

"Hey, don't pick a fight with me."

"Are you going to grate the cheese or not?"

A few more minutes go by. I need the cheese. Ron is now laying out an impeccable piece of wax paper on a cutting board, then measuring the hunk of cheese, trying to determine the proper hand grip.

"I need the cheese now! What are you doing?"

"I needed to prepare the surface, I couldn't just grate cheese onto the counter like this."

G. I. Gurdjieff, a Greek-Armenian philosopher in the early 20th century once described something he called The Law of Three. Everything happens in threes he said: positive, negative, neutral; active, passive, neutralizing; affirming, denying, reconciling, etc. Ron and I stand there, me holding my very sharp knife in my hand. He has the cheese. The tension mounts. Where is the third force in this moment? As if on cue, the sauce on the stove boils over spewing tomato all over. I run to turn it down. Ron quickly grabs a dishtowel and begins to wipe tomato splotches off the counter and the floor. A splatter lands on his head.

"Ow!"

I bend down to kiss his head. He stands up and wipes some tomato off of my face with the soiled rag. Love has prevailed again. The storm over, we sing together, "You say potato, and I say potato, you say tomato and I say tomato". We pause, toast with our cheap red wine and survey our beautiful, chaotic kitchen.

Ron's Potato Pancakes
Two generous servings

Growing up in a Polish/Russian household, I figured I had the goods on how to make the perfect potato pancakes. Ron is pretty much Wasp – Irish, Welsh, English, German. His culinary skills seemed to extend no further than a pie he had learned to make while an art student in Italy. So I was shocked to come home one night to find he was making potato pancakes from an old family recipe. Turns out the German side knew a thing or two about potatoes.

We have had many discussions over the merits of hand grated vs. grated by a food processor, coarsely grated vs. finely grated. The verdict is this. If you coarsely grate – either by hand or by food processor, you get a kind of gratin pancake. Many Jewish delis use this method, then deep fry the mixture. If you finely grate by hand, or purée the coarsely grated potato slightly, you get the old fashioned, heavy "placki" of the German/Polish variety, which are pan fried, not deep fried. My preferred method is to grate all the potatoes using the grating attachment on the food processor. Then I remove about 1/3 of the grated potatoes. I replace the blade with the purée blade, purée the remainder of the grated potatoes, then mix them in a bowl with the reserved grated potatoes. It gives a little texture to the batter.

3 eggs

2 tablespoons milk

2 tablespoons melted butter

2 tablespoons flour

3/4 tablespoon salt

1/8 tablespoon pepper

1 small onion, grated (much less painful if done in the food processor)

2 cups peeled raw grated potatoes

Condiments: Sour cream, yogurt and/or apple sauce or chutney

Mix all ingredients together. You can make either about 3 skillet size pancakes, or a bunch of little pancakes. Melt some butter in a frying pan. Fry, covered, on low heat till brown, between 3-7 minutes per side depending on size. Serve all with all the condiments you want.

Playing With Your Food

Substitutions:
You can use olive oil instead of butter if you are concerned about the dairy.
We have doubled the onion and added garlic for flavor variety.

Oops!:
I once forgot about the milk – I wondered why the mixture was so dry, but they still turned out OK.

Fire:
The trickiest part of this recipe is cooking the pancakes so that the potato mixture cooks thoroughly, without burning the outside. Depending on whether you make little pancakes or big ones will also affect your cooking time. Make sure they are not too thick. Keeping the lid on the pan will help cook the potatoes, but you should check the bottom. They are definitely not like breakfast pancakes.

Creamy Butternut Squash Risotto

Serves 6

You can vary the richness by the amount of Parmesan cheese you add at the end.

1 medium butternut squash, peeled, seeded and cut into chunks.

1/3 cup white wine

2 tablespoons butter, or 1 tablespoon butter, 1 tablespoon olive oil

1 medium onion, chopped

1 teaspoon chopped garlic

5 1/2 cups hot vegetable or chicken broth

2 cups arborio rice*

1 teaspoon chopped fresh rosemary

2 - 8 tablespoons grated Parmesan

Nutmeg, salt and pepper to taste

Steam squash until soft, about 10 minutes. Alternatively, you can throw the whole squash into the oven at 350 degrees, bake it for about 45 minutes (depending on size, it should be tender but not squishy to the touch). Remove the meat, discard the seeds. Purée. Set aside.

Sauté onion until soft, add garlic for another minute. Add rice and sauté, stirring till rice is well coated (about 1 minute). Add puréed squash. Add the wine and enough broth to cover the rice. Stir once. Bring to a boil, then lower heat to medium. When liquid is absorbed, add broth again, stir once again and let it cook till absorbed. Repeat this until your rice is soft. Sometimes, you need more liquid, sometimes less. If you need more, and your broth is salted, you may just want to add water at the end. This should take about 25 minutes. Remove from heat. Add rosemary, Parmesan, salt, pepper and nutmeg to taste.

Playing With Your Food

Substitutions:

This basic risotto recipe (minus the nutmeg) can be used with just about any vegetable/combo you want although with most other vegetables, you sauté them separately, then add at the end (except the onions of course!) People even use fruit, so mix it with anything you like!

Feel free to add more garlic if you are a garlic lover.

Oops:

The biggest fear people have with risotto is the adding of the liquid and the stirring. Unlike regular rice, you can stir to your heart's content.

Fire:

Don't be afraid to let the liquid evaporate almost to the very end each time. If by some chance, you accidentally pour all the liquid in at once, just let it boil. It will be more like flavored rice than risotto, but edible.

Layered Vegetable Terrine

Labor intensive, but the best terrine recipe I've found and Sooooo pretty

Terrine

2 cups shelled peas (or frozen)

2 cups chopped carrots

4 cups cauliflower florets

3 eggs separated

6 tablespoons low-fat or regular cream cheese

3 teaspoons lemon juice

1 tablespoons chopped fresh chives

2 tablespoons ground almonds

1/4 teaspoon freshly grated nutmeg

Salt and freshly ground white pepper

Salad

3 large peeled carrots

Small handful of snipped fresh chives

2 tablespoons hazelnut oil

1 teaspoon raspberry vinegar

Salt and freshly ground black pepper

Preheat the oven to 375 degrees. Lightly oil and line the bottom of a 2 lb. loaf pan with wax paper or parchment. Steam the peas, chopped carrots and cauliflower separately for 10 – 15 minutes. If you are using frozen peas, cook till just defrosted.

Let cool.

Purée the peas with 1 egg yolk, 2 tablespoons cream cheese, and 1 teaspoon lemon juice. Repeat with the carrots and then the cauliflower. Stir the chives into the pea purée, the almonds into the carrot purée, and the nutmeg into the cauliflower purée.

Whisk the egg whites until stiff, then carefully fold 1/3 into each purée until just combined. Season well and spoon the pea mousse into the prepared pan, carefully smoothing the surface.

Top with the carrot mousse and then the cauliflower mousse, smoothing the surface of each. Cover with a piece of lightly oiled wax paper.

Place the loaf pan in a roasting pan and pour in boiling water 2/3 of the way up the sides of the pan. Transfer to the oven and bake for 40 minutes. Remove the wax paper on top and cook for 10 –1 5 minutes more, until top feels firm to the touch. Remove from the oven and let cool in the pan on a wire rack.

Using a vegetable peeler, peel the whole carrots into thin strips and toss with the chives. Blend the oil, vinegar, and salt and pepper and mix with the carrot strips and chives.

Turn the terrine out of the pan and cut into slices. Serve on a plate, surrounded by the carrot salad.

Playing With Your Food

Guests:
This is a perfect dish for a dinner party where you want everyone to go "Ooooh!" It's also nice as an appetizer, but you may want to pre-slice and put it on little plates or crackers.

Substitutions:
Raspberry vinegar was an 80's fad, and sometimes when you buy it, it's been sweetened. Any infused berry vinegar is fine, and in a pinch, just white wine vinegar will work.

You don't really need the carrot salad, but it looks good.

It's also fun to serve the terrine with some kind of mayonnaise dressing.

Oops!
I admit, I was terrified the first time I made this. So many steps! Folding egg whites! Water in a roasting pan! The best way to look at this recipe is to think of it as a game. How much of a mess can I make? Look at those cool layers! Hey, this folding business is kind of cool. This is not a recipe to make when you are in a rush. It's really for a special event.

Food is Love

My siblings and I all share the same obsession for a full refrigerator. If there is the slightest space, we start to churn in anxiety. An insane fear boils up – I am going to starve to death. Both of our parents were in the Holocaust and endured long periods of starvation. When we were growing up, we were expected to eat everything on the table with gratitude. If we didn't like the disgusting, gushy baked eggplant, or the entire fish sitting on our plate, head and all, we received a lecture on starvation. "You have no idea how lucky you are. During the war, we were forced to eat worm soup and drink birch bark tea." This never seemed to increase our appetites. However, to this day, whenever I am attacked by any form of self-doubt, I instantly head for the refrigerator, if only to stare and reassure myself that no, I will not have to strip bark off trees this week.

One time, Ron and I did a juice fast. Ron wanted to cleanse, and I of course, wanted to lose weight. 8 days later, I was ready to kill someone and Ron had transcended all struggle on this planet and was floating on a cloud of bliss. He had lost fourteen pounds and I had gained one. Two days after breaking the fast, I gained another five pounds. It took over a year for my body to realize that we were not in a famine and I did not have to store every calorie.

What really nourishes us? There are people on this planet who call themselves Breatharians. They don't eat. One Breatharian who was interviewed explained that eating is a very inefficient way of receiving sustenance. After all, the food we eat comes from the sun and the air. So they go directly to the source, rising each morning and facing the rising sun. One man has claimed to have had no food for over a year.

People like Breatharians have proven that you can live a long time without food, but no one has yet claimed to be able to live without air. Does that make it food? The nice thing about air is that I don't have to buy it – yet. Entrepreneurs are already laying claim to this with everything from Oxygen Bars where people hang out with tubes in their noses inhaling… air, to bottled oxygen (only $4.95 a bottle for "free" oxygen.) How wonderful it is that the human capacity for ingenuity and commerce can be applied to our deteriorating atmosphere in such a creative fashion. If only we could find profit in just cleaning up the air we already have!

However, it's possible that even in the freshest of air, we don't all take in the same amount of sustenance. There are those of us who are living on barely enough air to sustain our existence. Taking rapid shallow breaths, tensing during inhale or exhale, congestion, and respiratory disease all affect the nutritional value of our air. A recent study showed that yoga practitioners had the same heart health as people who engaged in regular cardio exercise. Experts theorize that it is because yogis breathe so much more efficiently than the average person, they process more amounts of useful oxygen than a non-yogi.

One can live for a year without food, a few minutes without air, but I propose that there is another food even more essential. Call it life force, information, co-creation. Every second, we are processing (literally) information: visual, auditory, emotional, intellectual. From my joy at seeing the cardinal sitting on the branch outside the window, to my internal dialogue of self worth, to the label I read on the can of pasta sauce, I am being fed. What if everything around me is a kind of food? Music, ideas, smells, reactions: coming in, being digested, and then coming out as who we are. We know this in our deepest selves by the way we talk. "Mardi Gras is like a feast for the senses!" "There was so much information at that seminar it's going to take a week to digest it all." "I love that show, it's total mind candy!"

Joseph Chilton Pearce, the author of many books including the *Crack in the Cosmic Egg*, has called humans "novelty seeking organisms." We grow through taking in information. We literally grow a protein as children, called myelin, that sheaths our nerves. The protein *is* information. Everything a child takes in – Sponge Bob, Mom and Dad fighting, the taste of gushy eggplant, is food that coats the nerves and forms the responses of the future adult. If we denied the human being this essential food, the human will die. And if the human is fed a steady diet of junk food – sitcoms, inane conversations – the organism will reflect it just like junk food takes its toll on our health.

If everything around and within me is food, one could say my life is a banquet – feeding my being. An exquisite painting, a breath taking (aha!) sunset, the aroma of Ron's potato pancakes, an epiphany, a lover's phone call, a child's laugh, the sound of Mozart – perhaps it's not just music that is the food of love, but love itself can feed my soul – wow, real soul food! And I was worried about starving, while surrounded by abundance all around me.

Indonesian Vegetable Treat

Serves 4

4 tablespoons peanut or olive oil

8 oz. tofu, tempeh* or chicken

1 onion, chopped

1/2 cup diced eggplant

1 jalapeño pepper, seeded and minced

1/2 red bell pepper chopped

3 peeled chopped plum tomatoes (see note on peeling tomatoes, pg. 58)

2 cups chopped kale or spinach

1/2 cup chopped, peeled, steamed or baked butternut squash

2 tablespoons chopped basil (thai basil is best, but any basil will do) or cilantro

1 teaspoon salt

1/4 to 1/2 teaspoon Thai red curry paste (depending on heat)

1 tablespoon maple syrup

1/2 cup coconut milk

1 tablespoon lime juice

1/4 cup roasted, chopped cashews

Lime wedges

If you are using tempeh, cut the tempeh into bite size pieces and steam them for 15 minutes. If you are using tofu or chicken, cut into bite size pieces. Heat 2 tablespoons of oil over moderately high heat. When it is hot but not smoking, fry chicken, tofu, or tempeh until browned. Remove from pan and drain on paper towels. Discard oil.

Heat remainder of oil. Add onions till softened. Add jalapeño and eggplant, sauté till eggplant starts to soften, add red peppers. Add tomatoes, cook until water is almost absorbed. Add remaining vegetables, herbs, salt, curry paste, maple syrup and coconut milk . Cook for 10 – 15 minutes, add lime juice and stir till sauce thickness is to your liking. Adjust seasonings, add tempeh, tofu or chicken and heat through. Serve over rice, noodles or even cooked potatoes. Sprinkle cashews on top and garnish with lime wedge.

Playing With Your Food
Substitutions:
Using the onion as your base, feel free to experiment with vegetables. This is a perfect dish for cleaning out your vegetable bin – string beans, zucchini, red cabbage are just a few suggestions for substitutions in this recipe.

I have made this recipe without either basil or cilantro – it's not the end of the world!

No red curry paste? Throw in some hot sauce!

No lime? Use lemon.

SALADS AND VEGETABLE SIDE DISHES

To make a good salad is to be a brilliant diplomatist—
the problem is entirely the same in both cases.
To know exactly how much oil one must put with one's vinegar.
— Oscar Wilde

Standing on Your Own Two Feet

Perhaps the biggest challenge for the committed cook is staying comfortable while standing. Any number of aches and pains can be traced to just standing over the chopping block, the stove and the sink. The feet get sore, the back aches, the neck gets stiff.

Let's look at some reasons for the discomfort. First of all, the human skeleton was not designed to stand. It was designed for movement. Running, walking, bending, reaching; these are the skeleton's great talents. If we were meant to stand still, why would nature have perched up to six plus feet of mass on two tiny points? The feet and ankles cannot hold you up indefinitely. In fact, that's really the reason the Palace Guards at Buckingham Palace periodically keel over. It's not the heat. Enforced stillness affects the circulatory system. Boom.

Of course, when you are chopping, stirring or rinsing, you are not absolutely still, so the odds of crashing are small. However, the effort to stay in place remains the main message to your nervous system. So sometimes, even though you move from one task to another, the back and legs remain tense. Following are a few things you can try to reduce discomfort in your legs. You may find that doing these movements also relieves back tension as well.

1) The Heel Bounce. Place your hands onto your counter. Bring your feet to a parallel stance about hip width apart. Raise yourself up a bit on your toes, then let your heels bounce onto the floor, immediately letting your heels come up again. Create a rhythm, boom, boom, boom. You don't have to bounce hard or smash your heels, make it light but definite, about 20 times. Let your knees be soft, don't lock them.

Then shift your weight onto your left leg. Bounce your right heel up and down without putting any weight on it. Shift your weight and do the same to the left foot, taking a little rest in between each movement. When you bounce with the individual foot, let your knee bend and see if you can get your heel going really fast.

2) Charleston Feet. If you need to, you can hold on to the counter. Arrange your feet in a parallel position again. Shift your weight to your left side. Leaving your right heel in place, turn your foot out to the right, then return. As you move, sense what is happening in your hip. Can your pelvis move? What do you feel in your back? Speed it up, slow it down. Rest a moment, then do the other leg. Rest. Shift your weight again to the left. This time, leave the ball of the foot where it is, and move your right heel to the right and then back. Can you speed that up? What happens to your hips? Your pelvis? After resting, do the same thing on the left side. For extra fun, try moving both sets of toes apart and together, and speed that up. Now do the same thing with your heels. For a real brain teaser, alternate the toes and heels.

3) Toe/Heel Rock. Place one foot comfortably in front of the other. Rock your weight onto your forward foot and pick up your back heel, then rock back onto

your back foot and pick up the ball of the front foot. You can do it with straight legs, bent knees and just relaxed knees. See how each choice for your knees affects the movement. Shift forward and back several times. What changes the weight? Can you sense your knees? Can you initiate the movement from your pelvis? Switch your legs. This position can be quite useful when kneading dough, because it gives more power to your arms than simply standing legs apart and knees locked.

Asian Chicken/Tofu Salad

Serves 2

This is great with leftover chicken .

1 cup cooked chicken in bite size pieces or 1 cup of tofu - either raw or fried - see note.

2 cups mixed salad greens - whatever you've got

2 scallions chopped

1/2 cup bean sprouts (optional)

2 tablespoons cashews or peanuts - either pre-roasted, or raw cashews toasted in a 350°oven for 6 -8 minutes

Dressing:

2 tablespoons tahini*

2 tablespoons peanut butter

1 clove garlic

2 tablespoons rice vinegar

1 teaspoon sweetener - sugar, honey, or agave syrup*

1 tablespoon Tamari or soy sauce

1 tablespoon toasted sesame oil

1/2 teaspoon hot chili oil (optional)

Note on tofu: While it's true that frying changes the nature of fat from a "good" fat to a "bad" fat, I believe it's only harmful if it's a daily diet done in excess. There are those who say that a quick fry actually seals in nutrients, so go figure. To fry tofu, you need about 1/4 inch of oil in your pan or a bit more in your wok. Heat the oil to hot but not smoking. It's best if you slice your tofu and press the liquid out on a clean cloth or with paper towels, then cut into cubes. If you don't, it will spatter as the water gets cooked out, so have a spatter pan handy. You fry it till it's crispy on all sides. It really takes the chalkiness out of the flavor.

For the dressing, mix all ingredients together and taste. If you need more tang, add more vinegar. If it's too thick, add a little water. You can serve it a couple of ways – you can pour the dressing over just the chicken, toss and coat well, then arrange it on top of the combined vegetables. Or you can mix all the salad ingredients together with the chicken or tofu and serve the dressing on the side.

Playing With Your Food

Substitutions:
If you have no tahini, just use 4 tablespoons peanut butter
No rice vinegar? Use white wine vinegar

Baked Yams and Apples with Maple Glaze
Makes 8 servings.

3 large garnet yams, peeled and sliced into 1/4 inch rounds.
3 cooking apples, peeled, cored and sliced in 1/4 inch wedges.
3/4 cup maple syrup
1/2 cup apple cider
Salt and pepper to taste.

Preheat oven to 350 degrees. Arrange yams and apples in a 9 x 13 baking dish or casserole in alternating layers. In a saucepan, bring syrup and cider to a boil; remove from heat. Pour over yams and apples. Sprinkle with salt and pepper.

Cover baking dish with foil, bake 1 hour. Uncover, bake until yams are soft and syrup is thick, about 15 - 20 minutes.

Playing With Your Food

Guests:

Have no fear about bringing this as your covered dish offering for Thanksgiving – it will please the traditionalists as well as those longing for a slightly different take on yams.

Substitutions:

Any apple is just fine if "cooking" apples are unavailable

If you have no maple syrup, substitute 1/2 cup of brown sugar and 1/4 cup of water.

Fire:

Keep your eye on the baking after you remove the aluminum foil, it thickens quickly and then can stick to the pan.

Grilled Eggplant with Pistachio and Mint Salsa
6 -8 servings.

This recipe is the original reason for this book. Every year, someone calls and asks for it. It comes from a book, now out of print, called The Inspired Vegetarian by Louise Pickford, not to be confused by any other book with the same title. When I opened the book to copy this recipe, it automatically opened to this page, which was covered by a Jackson Pollack abstract of ingredients I've spilled on the book over the years.

Oil for frying

2 medium to large eggplants or 5 small Japanese eggplants

Salt

Salsa:

1/4 cup shelled pistachio nuts. (Sometimes it's a challenge to find unsalted pistachios. In these situations, I rinse them, then taste the salsa before adding salt. It seems to work out fine)

1/2 cup loosely packed mint leaves

1/4 cup loosely packed parsley leaves

1 clove coarsely chopped garlic

2 scallions, trimmed and coarsely chopped

3/4 cup olive oil

2 tablespoons white wine vinegar

1/4 teaspoon sugar

Salt and freshly ground pepper

Slice the eggplants about 1/2 inch thick. If you are using the small eggplants, just slice in half lengthwise. Sprinkle with salt. Let them drain on racks or paper towels for 30 minutes.

Blanch the pistachio nuts in boiling water for 30 seconds. Refresh under cold water, drain well and pat dry. Rub the nuts in a clean dish towel to remove their skins. I wish I could say that all you have to do is roll them around in the towel, but often you have to rub each nut to get those pesky skins off.

Blend the nuts, mint, parsley, garlic and scallions in food processor to form a fairly smooth paste. Stir in the remaining ingredients and let infuse.

Preheat the broiler if you are not grilling.

Wash the eggplants thoroughly and dry well. Brush with oil and place under broiler or on grill until nice and brown. Turn over, brush with more oil and broil till this side browns. **Note:** It is really important that the eggplant be tender. You should be able to stick a fork in and it almost feels like it will fall apart. Arrange the eggplants on a platter and spoon some of the salsa on them. Leave the rest of the salsa in a small bowl with a spoon for those guests who fall in love with the flavor.

Playing With Your Food

Guests:
This is definitely a party dish; you end up with a lot of sauce! In fact, you could easily add another eggplant to the grill.

Fire:
Whether you are broiling or grilling, it's a quick turn from perfectly cooked to blackened, so be vigilant.

Thought for Food

It's 3:57AM. I shuffle toward the bathroom in the dark trying to keep my eyes half closed so that my return to the covers will immediately return me to dreamland. I know I have to go to the bathroom when I start dreaming about toilets in the middle of people's kitchens. They say that dreams are messages from home. These dreams are messages from my bladder.

As I stumble back to bed, I realize with horror that my mind is planning dinner for Friday night. We are not having guests. It is not a special occasion. I don't need to plan dinner three days in advance. But here I am, in the middle of the night, mentally pulling beans out of the freezer, thinking about whether I want to use coconut milk or go for Mexican.

I have a deep wish for spiritual enlightenment, and have studied many techniques for stilling the mind. For the last thirty years, I've sat each morning on my

83

cushion, trying to be present to what is. And then suddenly, my mind is busily chopping red peppers and mushrooms for an omelet, or trying to figure out if yogurt would be a good substitute for buttermilk in the pancakes. I return to my breath, in, out, I am here, I am here, and then... I'm frying bacon.

I have friends who forget to eat. Imagine. Others think that cooking is a waste of time; why go through all that trouble when you can pick up something perfectly good at the health food store? I've tried it. I stand in front of the deli counter: kale with tamari dressing, hijiki salad, grilled salmon, curried chicken salad. And instead of buying, I find myself thinking, "I have lemon and tamari at home. A little fresh garlic and I could have a gourmet wilted kale dish in minutes. And why should I pay $3.00 for a hijiki salad that's been sitting there all afternoon, and would only cost me 50 cents to make fresh?" etc, etc till I walk away empty handed to go home and cook dinner.

When we were growing up, we'd long for the foods we saw on TV: Chef Boyardee, Wonder Bread, Wish Bone Salad Dressing. My parents insisted that this was "junk food." So far ahead of their time, they seemed crazy, my Mom insisted on baking the bread and my Dad taught me to make salad dressing. "You see, it would cost $1.50 for this dressing at the store. And look, a few cents worth of vinegar, some oil, some spices and you have it fresh!" To this day, I make my own salad dressing.

Can I blame this on my Dad? After all, one of our favorite pastimes is to blame our parents. Why not obsessive cooking? One of his favorite expressions was, "Some people eat to live. I live to eat!" I have even inherited his gift for food stains. Whether I'm cooking, or eating, I can always be sure that if I am wearing good clothes, and especially white, that it will attach itself to my garment. Same with Dad. Not a meal goes by where he doesn't drop some gravy, a piece of chicken or sauce on his shirt.

For a short time after the War, my Dad had fast talked his way into a job as head pastry chef at a hotel in London, even though he'd never baked a cake in his life. He used to speak about the terror he felt as he walked around, approving and disapproving various cakes, dividing his free time between trying to think up inventive pastries and trying to seduce the female staff. Scientists have been saying that our DNA doesn't just carry our hair and skin color and height information. They tell us that our responses to events are also carried in our DNA. Perhaps my parents' experiences during the war and my father's chef adventure got imprinted into me so that I was born thinking about food.

I am not alone. I was once having dinner with another friend who is a compulsive chef. He sighed. "I wake up in the morning thinking about a particularly satisfying stock reduction I made three years ago, or try to figure out whether it's worth driving 30 miles to the seafood market because I'm thinking scallops are just what's needed for tonight. Even as I'm eating a meal, my mind is thinking about things I can do with the leftovers."

Does imagination have calories? Is it possible that my thoughts can put on weight? Oh no! Could these very imaginings be my obstacle to enlightenment *and* sleekness? I think of the Spartan meals I've seen in monasteries, the streamlined menus at Zen retreats. You don't see chocolate pecan pie there, no chicken with tarragon mayonnaise, no black bean cakes with mango salsa. Creative frenzy is contained, a serene garden, a lovely chapel, perhaps some secret journaling on the part of the monks. But wait! Could there be another way? Another path to inner transformation and a slender shape? The way of the chef?

That's it! Instead of fighting it, food could become my mantra! My inner chatter could become my inner chant – I just need to make it intentional. After all, it's not about the thought, it's about the thinker. I could even turn it into an inner Gregorian Chant (join me now in singing):

How about a smoothie?

I think there are still straw… berries

Is the yogurt still good

Pineapple is going… bad

By intentionally thinking about food, perhaps I'll think a little slower, chew my mental meals more carefully, digest it better. I'll be thinner and more present. I will be like my Dad – I will live to eat, even my thoughts.

Kale with Tamari Dressing

Serves 2 - 4

Sometimes you can sauté kale and it tastes delicious, sometimes, (I'm sure a food scientist could tell me the reason) it comes out tough. A foolproof method is to steam the kale and then add the dressing.

One bunch kale (about 8 large leaves), coarsely chopped

Dressing:

4 tablespoons Olive oil

2 -3 cloves garlic, minced

Juice of 1/2 lemon (about 1/4 cup)

2 tablespoons tamari sauce*

2 tablespoons toasted sesame oil

Steam the kale till it is wilted. Put into bowl. Sauté the garlic in 2 tablespoons of the olive oil. Mix together lemon, tamari. Keep whisking as you add the oils and garlic (with its oil). Pour over the warm kale, toss well.

Playing With Your Food

Substitutions:
You can use any green – mustard, spinach, even green beans with this dressing. You just need to adjust your amounts according to their "shrink" factor.
Any kind of soy sauce will do.
If you leave out the Tamari and Sesame Oil, and just add salt, it's still delicious, then you

call it Mediterranean Kale.

No time to sauté the garlic? Put it through a garlic press raw – it's zingy but delicious.

Oops!

If you pour all the dressing ingredients together, you just have to whisk again before you pour because it won't homogenize as well.

Braised Red Cabbage in Wine and Port
8 servings

1 tablespoon olive oil

1 large onion, thinly sliced

1 1/2 lb red cabbage, finely shredded (the grating attachment in the food processor works great for this)

1 tablespoon chopped fresh thyme

1 teaspoon caraway seeds

10 juniper berries, crushed

3/4 cup red wine

1/4 cup ruby port wine

1 cup walnut halves

1/ 2 cup golden raisins

2 tablespoons of red wine vinegar

Salt and freshly ground pepper

Heat the oil in a large skillet and sauté the onion for 5 minutes, until soft. Stir in the cabbage, thyme, caraway seeds and juniper berries and sauté for 5 minutes more.

Add the wines and vinegar; cover and simmer gently for 20 minutes. Add the walnuts and raisins, cover and simmer for 10 to 15 minutes more, until the cabbage is tender. If you find that the cabbage is still not tender and the liquid is cooked out, add another 1/4 cup port, or red wine or a mixture to it.

Adjust the seasonings and serve hot.

Playing With Your Food

Substitutions:

You can substitute ¼ teaspoon dried thyme for the fresh.

If you have no caraway or juniper, the dish will still taste fine, just not as complex. It's worth buying these ingredients. One time I went outside and grabbed cedar berries off of a neighbor's tree.

Any port wine will do.

Any raisins will do.

Fire:

I have often found, for some reason, I run out of liquid before the cabbage seems done. Feel free to add more red wine.

Cucumber Salad with Lime

Serves 6 - 8

1 3/4 lbs cucumbers

2 teaspoons kosher salt

2 limes

1 teaspoon white wine or tarragon vinegar

4 cloves garlic, gently smashed and peeled

1/2 teaspoon sugar

1/4 teaspoon ground coriander

1 teaspoon salt

1 tablespoon chopped Italian parsley

Peel the cucumbers and cut off the ends. Slice the cucumbers in half lengthwise and with a teaspoon, scrape out the pulp and seeds. Many people complain about cucumbers giving them indigestion. It's really the seeds that are the culprits. Slice each half crosswise into crescents 1/4 inch thick. Place in a sieve, sprinkle with the Kosher salt, toss to distribute the salt. Drain for 30 minutes. (The salt will draw out any excess water and bitterness that later could affect the dressing.) To insure dryness, pat or roll the cucumbers dry on or between paper towels or cloth napkins.

With a vegetable peeler, remove the zest from the lime very carefully, taking as little white pith as possible. Cut the peel into very fine strips until you have about 1/2 teaspoon. Soften both limes by rolling them on a table with your palm; they will release their juices more easily this way. Squeeze out the juice; you should have at least 2 tablespoons.

Toss the cucumbers and lime juice together with the remaining ingredients except the salt and parsley. Refrigerate, covered, for at least 30 minutes. Before serving, remove the garlic and add the salt and parsley.

Playing With Your Food

Guests:
This is a wonderful dish for a party.

Substitutions:
Regular salt is fine if you don't have Kosher salt
Lemon works fine, although the lime gives it a distinctive flavor

---

Curried Rice Salad
Serves 8

I cannot remember a party where I did not serve this. Nor a party where someone did not ask for this recipe. This rice salad is traditionally made with white rice. But I have always used brown rice in it, and no one has ever complained. I actually think it tastes better this way, but feel free to use white rice if you prefer.

1 1/2 cups long grained brown rice

3 1/2 cups water or chicken stock

1 1/2 teaspoons salt

1/2 cup julienne strips of carrot

1/2 cup julienne strips of white part of leek

1 teaspoon medium-hot curry powder

1/4 teaspoon ground cumin

1/4 teaspoon minced garlic

2 heaping teaspoons grated red radishes

3 tablespoons pine nuts, toasted in a preheated 350 degree oven for 5 - 10 minutes, until golden

1/3 cup raisins

2 tablespoons freshly squeezed lime juice

1 tablespoon red-wine vinegar

2 tablespoons soy oil

1 tablespoon chopped parsley

1 teaspoon minced fresh dill

2 tablespoons thinly sliced scallion

2 heaping tablespoons chutney (like Major Grey's or Green Tomato - see page 00)

Bring water or stock, rice and salt to boil, reduce to simmer. Cook until rice is tender but still firm. There may be a little water left. Don't let it overcook. If there is water left, drain it in a sieve and rinse under cool water to stop the cooking. Or take it off a little earlier and let it sit in the sieve, letting it cook out the juices, and don't rinse.

Place rice in mixing bowl. Add everything to the rice. Toss well and serve warm or slightly chilled.

Playing With Your Food

Substitutions:
While this recipe is worth going through the trouble of buying the ingredients, you certainly can swap out the vinegars, nuts, and lime juice.

Oops!:
I've forgotten to buy radish and dill and it still tasted OK.
The raisins were not in the original recipe – I had accidentally turned the page in the book and saw raisins, threw them in, then realized my mistake. I served it anyway. After that party, people kept asking for the recipe for that "rice salad that had the raisins in it" so I left it in!

A Sense of Scale

I've decided to have a party. You know, a resplendent feast of savory foods I never have time to make in daily life, a room full of people who don't know each other, festive decorations – all squeezed in between renovating my living room, going to other people's holiday parties, and a full time job.

I'm going to prepare a curried rice salad in advance that involves huge amounts of julienned carrots and leeks and grated radishes. To grate and julienne by hand will take forever and I only have my one-hour lunch break. My food processor is broken so I dash to my sister's and pilfer hers. The 10 minutes it takes to rifle her cabinets, find all the attachments is well worth the time, no?

I get home and set it up, ram the carrots through in record time. I grab the grating attachment blade to remove it. It won't budge. It's the same food processor as mine, just larger. It should be the same, right? Maybe it's just suction. I try to loosen one side. It doesn't budge. I squeeze my fingers under the cutting blades and try to pull up from the center, succeeding only in bruising all my fingers on the sharp edges of the blade.

Visions of sledge hammers start dancing in my head. "It's not yours," I tell myself, "You'd better not break it." I release the bowl and try to pull the attachment up with the bowl. I look at the clock. I could have julienned a pound of carrots by hand in the time it's taking to struggle with this. I'm sweating. My face is red. I begin to curse the machine. I become my father struggling with the lawn mower, fighting with his dying car, battling the vacuum cleaner. Sweat pours down my face. I'm going to be late for work. But I cannot let this machine triumph over me. I go downstairs and get a chisel. Slowly, painstakingly, I work the chisel around the stem, trying to loosen the attachment. I'm muttering incoherent commentary on the uselessness of trying to save time; that the machines of the world have conspired against me; that I went to college in order to be on my knees chiseling the food processor.

For some reason, Madonna floats into my head. I think to myself, "Is this why I never became rich and famous, among the greats? Because I spend too much time wasting my time with time-saving devices? I mean, would Madonna be sitting here chiseling her food processor? No! She'd be twisted in an exotic ashtanga yoga pose that ensures her perpetual youth, or be busy envisioning her final album before she begins another career writing children's books. She has a cook using the food processor. No, her cook probably juliennes vegetables by hand. He chants power mantras as he meticulously cuts each perfect carrot sliver as an act of devotion to his guru, knowing he is well paid for his perfect vegetables. I can't afford a cook. But wait. Madonna wasn't always rich. She began as a struggling young performer." Perhaps greatness requires that you sacrifice the food processor and only eat take out.

But then I think of Martha Stewart, who can probably take apart a food processor and put it back together in less time than it takes me to find the scattered parts in the corners of my kitchen cabinet. Not only that, she could probably finish this rice salad, make a wreath and design a new line of towels for K–Mart during this short lunch break.

I begin to feel very small. The hugeness of my insignificance looms over me as if a camera was zooming from a close-up of my hand around the blade to a wide shot of the kitchen, zooming upward over my house, now a dot among other house dots, ever upward, revealing the sea of humanity, and eventually, the famous shot of the globe from space. If I disappeared in this instant, it would not affect the universe one iota. If the rice salad doesn't get done, if the party gets cancelled, if Madonna's next album bombs, if Martha Stewart gets arrested again, none of it ultimately matters. I feel a moment of profound kinship with both Madonna and Martha.

Suddenly, the blade releases. It slides off as if I have pushed a magic button, no effort, no secret password. I dump the carrots into the salad bowl. Without a second thought, I replace the blade, grate the radishes, and go to remove the blade. It's stuck again. Martha, where are you?

Lentil and Sweet Pepper Salad

Serves 6 -8.

3 bell peppers - vary the color - 1 red, 1 yellow, 1 orange

1 1/4 cups lentils, washed

3 cups water

1 small onion, peeled

1 clove garlic, peeled

1 small red chili pepper, seeded and finely chopped

1 small red onion, thinly sliced

1/2 cup dried apricots, thinly sliced

Salt and freshly ground pepper

Dressing:

1/4 cup olive oil

Juice of one lemon

2 cloves garlic, crushed

1 tablespoon chopped cilantro

1 tablespoon chopped parsley

2 teaspoons cumin

Salt and freshly ground pepper

Heat the broiler. Broil the peppers until charred and blistered on all sides. Tie in a plastic bag or place in a covered dish and let cool to loosen skins.

Put the lentils, water, onion and garlic into a 2-quart saucepan. Bring to a boil, lower the heat, and simmer, uncovered, for 20 – 25 minutes, or until the lentils are tender but still a little crunchy. This is key. If you cook them till they're soft, they keep cooking and turn to mush in the salad. Drain and place in a large bowl.

Meanwhile, make the dressing. Blend the oil, lemon juice, garlic, cilantro, parsley and cumin, and season with salt and pepper. Drain the lentils, discard the onion and garlic and place the lentils in a large bowl. Stir in the dressing and set aside.

Peel and seed the bell peppers over a bowl to catch any juices, slice the flesh thinly and reserve. Pour any juices into the lentils and leave to cool completely.

Stir the bell peppers, chili pepper, onion, apricot slices and salt and pepper to taste into the lentils and serve.

Playing With Your Food

Guests:

Choose your guests wisely – some people have issues with any kind of legumes. Vegetarians love this dish.

Substitutions:

You can leave out the cilantro

If you don't have a red chili pepper, a jalapeño is fine.

Yellow or white onions are also fine, just not as colorful.

Fire:

If you overcook the lentils, save them for soup. Nothing is ever wasted.

Green Beans with Pears, Pine Nuts, and Chèvre

Serves 4 - 6

3/4 lb young green beans, ends removed

1 1/2 ripe pears (Bosc or Anjou tend to hold shape best)

1/3 cup pine nuts, toasted for 7 - 10 minutes in a preheated 350 degree oven

Vinaigrette:

1 tablespoon white wine vinegar

1 1/2 teaspoons lemon juice

1 1/2 teaspoons Dijon mustard

1/2 teaspoon salt

1/4 teaspoon freshly ground pepper

1/2 cup oil (olive, soy)

1/4 cup moist chèvre (goat) cheese, crumbled.

Blanch the beans in boiling salted water for 1 1/2 minutes, or steam till just getting soft. Drain in a colander and place under cold running water, or plunge into ice water until cool. This keeps them bright green. Allow to drain thoroughly. Pat dry.

Halve and core the pears and slice lengthwise 1/4 inch thick. Combine the beans, pears, and pine nuts in a mixing bowl.

To make the vinaigrette, place all the ingredients except the oil and chèvre in a mixing bowl or large cup. With a small or medium whisk, or even a fork, combine thoroughly, using a rapid wrist motion. While whisking, add the oils, in a slow steady steam, incorporating them slowly to guarantee that the dressing emulsifies.

Note:This vinaigrette is a wonderful, basic dressing for any kind of salad. As you pour, you may find you need less than the recipe calls for, you can always use the leftovers in another salad.

Pour dressing over bean mixture, and sprinkle chèvre on top. Toss gently. If you can't serve it right away, keep it in the refrigerator.

Playing With Your Food

Substitutions:
Any vinegar will do in this dressing, although mild is better
If you don't have chevre, you can use a combo of feta and cream cheese.
Walnuts are a fine substitution for pine nuts in a pinch.

Oops:
Made too much? The leftovers are fine for a day or two.

Fire:
Keep an eye on the pine nuts. Depending on your oven, they can be done in even less than 7 minutes and if you just wait till 10, you may have black nuts.

The Ultimate Tabbouleh
Serves 4
2 cups boiling water
1 cup bulgur wheat*
2 cloves garlic, minced
1/2 cup lemon juice
1/4 cup olive oil
1/4 teaspoon salt
1/4 - 1/2 cup chopped parsley
2 tablespoons chopped mint
2 scallions chopped
1 -2 tomatoes, diced

Pour boiling water into bowl; add bulgur, garlic, lemon juice, salt and oil. Let it sit till water is absorbed, about 45 minutes. If you have a food processor, you can save a lot of time by puréeing the parsley and mint. Add the rest of ingredients, toss well.

Playing With Your Food

Guests:
People think all tabbouleh tastes the same because they're used to picking this up at the deli counter. This recipe is so good (and so easy), it's perfect to bring to a party or potluck. Everyone is always stunned at the flavor!

Substitutions:
You can add more parsley; in some Middle Eastern versions, there is more parsley than bulgur.
This is a perfectly tasty salad if you use any similarly shaped grain: cous cous, quinoa*, even pasta.

Butternut Squash Purée with Coconut

Serves 4 - 6

1 large butternut squash (about 1 lb), baked or steamed

4 tablespoons unsalted butter

2 teaspoons fennel seeds, crushed

1/2 teaspoon cardamom seeds, crushed (See note)

2 -3 tablespoons maple syrup

3 tablespoons cream (optional)

1 -2 teaspoons hot green chilies, seeded and minced

1 teaspoon salt

1/4 cup shredded unsweetened coconut and/or chopped hazelnuts, toasted in a 300 degree oven until golden

2 tablespoons lime juice

Note on Cardamom Seeds: They are usually sold still in their pods. It's often ridiculously labor intensive to open these pods and get the seeds out in order to crush them. I've found that it's really simple to throw a few pods into a mortar and pestle, smash them a few times, then just pick out the pieces of pod. Then you can easily crush the seeds – either with the mortar and pestle or with a coffee grinder.

To steam the squash, peel it, remove the seeds, and cut into cubes. Steam till tender. If it has been baked whole, cut open the squash, scoop out the seeds and fibers. Place pulp or steamed cubes into food processor or bowl. Mash into purée with potato masher, or process till puréed.

Heat 3 tablespoons of the butter in a 12-inch nonstick frying pan over moderate heat. When it is hot and frothing, add the fennel seeds, cardamom seeds and green chilies. Within seconds add the squash purée, maple syrup, cream if desired and salt. Cook, stirring frequently, until thickened—about

5 minutes. Before serving, garnish with toasted coconut and/or hazelnuts, the remaining butter (if desired) and sprinkle with lime juice.

Playing With Your Food

Substitutions:
If you have no fennel seeds, it still tastes fine
Ground cardamom is just fine.
Lemon instead of lime juice works.
In a pinch, you can use brown sugar instead of maple syrup.

Oops:
I once threw everything in the frying pan at once – not as toasty, but perfectly edible.

Fire:
Watch your nuts and/or coconut. It's also good to give then a stir or shake to distribute color.

Mexican Salad
Serves 3 - 4
2 red bell peppers
1 cup cooked beans – black beans are traditional, but any beans work
2 scallions, chopped
1 jalapeño, seeded and minced
2 cups cooked corn
1/2 cup pitted, halved Kalamata or whole Niçoise olives
3 tablespoons finely chopped cilantro or parsley or a combination of the two
1 clove garlic, minced
Juice of 1 lemon
Salt and pepper
1/4 cup olive oil

Heat the broiler. Broil the peppers until charred and blistered on all sides. Tie in a plastic bag or place in a covered dish and let cool to loosen skins (about 10 minutes).

While the peppers are sweating, put beans, corn, scallions, olives and herbs in a bowl and mix together. In a separate bowl or cup mix together lemon, garlic, salt and pepper, then add oil in a slow stream while whisking till it's emulsified.

Peel the peppers, discard the seeds and cut into small strips. Add to vegetable mix. Pour dressing on and toss well.

Playing With Your Food

Substitutions:
This recipe was originally created with leftovers. You can have fun with any combination of beans and vegetables. Shredded summer squash, red onions instead of scallions, chopped fresh tomatoes are just a few possibilities.

Fire:
Make sure you remember to turn the peppers so that all sides are equally blackened.

SAUCES AND CONDIMENTS

Mayonnaise: One of the sauces which serve
the French in place of a state religion.
— Ambrose Bierce

England has forty-two religions and only two sauces.
— Voltaire

Cranberry Chutney

Makes about 2 pints

This is an excellent addition to turkey and chicken – a great alternative to cranberry sauce for the holidays

12 oz cranberries

3/4 cup brown sugar

1/3 cup raisins

1/2 cup chopped dried pears

1 large, crisp apple, peeled, cored and chopped

1/4 cup chopped onion

1/3 cup cider vinegar

2 tablespoons peeled and finely chopped fresh ginger root

Grated zest of 1 lemon

Pinch of salt

1 1/2 cup water, more if needed

1 1/2 teaspoons whole mustard seed

1 - 2 small hot red chiles, dried or fresh

Rinse the berries and pick them over, discarding any that are soft and brown. In a large pot, combine the berries with all but the last two ingredients, and bring everything to a slow boil, stirring to dissolve the sugar.

Toast the mustard seeds in a small pan, shaking them over medium heat until they begin to pop and jump. Toast the chilies in a very hot pan or directly over a flame until they blister and turn black in spots, then mince them. This is a little tricky. Sometimes the chiles are so thin that when you put them directly on the flame, they disintegrate, especially the dried ones. Stir the mustard and minced chile into the cranberry mixture.

Lower the heat and simmer the chutney for about an hour, stirring occasionally, adding a little more water if the chutney becomes too thick and threatens to scorch.

The chutney can be kept refrigerated and covered for several weeks or put into canning jars and processed in a hot water bath for longer storage. Flavor improves after a day or two.

Playing With Your Food

Guests:

Needless to say, there will always be people who ask, "Where is the REAL cranberry sauce?" Cook this for your own delight and there will always be fans.

Substitutions:

A pear instead of an apple is fine.

If you have no fresh ginger, go ahead and add a teaspoon of powdered. It's not the same, but not bad.

Fire:

When the mustard seeds start to pop they start to leap out of the pan. If you have a spatter screen, it keeps them under control. I usually put a few extra in the pan and don't try to capture the escapees.

Be careful when blackening those chiles: don't inhale the fumes!

The Alchemy of the Self

I have read that the ancient alchemists' quest to turn lead into gold was a metaphor for inner work that transformed the human into a higher order of being. Cooking can be approached from the same perspective: a number of individual elements blending together to become greater than the sum of their parts. What first is just a list of ingredients becomes a chutney, a sauce or a cake. Likewise, there's an alchemy taking place in ourselves with every action. Reaching, turning, walking, stirring, chopping are all complex actions that require a blending of different ingredients in the human movement vocabulary. When you chop, you are involving not just your hand and arm. Your eyes, thoughts, back, stance, breath and more are working together in the magical act called chopping.

While waiting for a pot of vegetables to transform itself into a sauce, you can try the following movement study we ordinarily call stirring. You may find that this seemingly mechanical action is rich with possibilities for self knowledge and better use of self.

As you stir, begin to pay attention to the weight under your feet. Can you sense how it is distributed? Is it more on one foot than on the other? Is the weight on the outsides, insides, balls or heels of the feet? Is it the same on each foot? Can you keep stirring and at the same time, shift your weight in different ways - forward and back, side to side. How do your knees feel as you do this? Are you still able to stir as you pay attention to another part of yourself? Stop everything for a moment. It might even be good to walk around the kitchen or take a seat.

The next time you go to stir, notice your pelvis. Your pelvis connects your legs to your spine. As you stir, do you notice any movement there? Or is it being held still? Are you clenching your buttocks? Do you need to? What about your low back? Many people grip in the low back while executing the simplest task - an old childhood habit based on fear of falling.

What would happen if you circle your pelvis as you stir? Are you circling your pelvis in the same direction as your spoon or in the opposite direction? Can you change directions? Take another rest.

When you return to stirring, notice where you are looking. Are you staring into the pan? Do your eyes feel relaxed? Try to move your eyes slowly right and left while you stir. You can do it with your face down, looking at the pan, or you can pick your head up in line with the horizon. Notice what happens to your stirring if you are not looking at the pan. What do you feel in your neck? In the back of your head? Make sure you take many small rests when moving the eyes. We have a tendency to do more than is necessary with the really small movements. Take another break.

When you return to stirring, notice your arm and hand. What is the level of tension in your grip? Notice the shoulder of the arm that is stirring. Now, switch your hands and stir with your non-habitual hand. One of the best ways to keep the brain active and the body balanced is to interrupt our habits. We can experiment best when we are in a safe environment. For a few minutes, feel how this hand and arm respond to the act of stirring. As you stir with this hand, what else are you able to sense: in your eyes, pelvis, legs and feet? Now go back to your habitual arm.

By now your sauce is probably quite smooth! But if you still need a little more stirring, or a bit of a brain challenge, see if you can stir your sauce while shifting your weight, circling your pelvis, moving your eyes right and left. Make sure you're still breathing!

You may find, after trying this, that you have a new relationship with stirring as well as greater awareness of how you use yourself in other activities.

Green Tomato or Apple Chutney

Makes about 3 pints

1 seeded chopped lemon

1 clove peeled, chopped garlic

5 cups firm peeled chopped apples or green tomatoes

2 1/4 cups brown sugar

1 1/2 cups raisins

3 oz chopped crystallized ginger or 1/4 cup peeled, chopped fresh ginger

1 1/2 teaspoons salt

1/4 teaspoon cayenne

2 cups cider vinegar

2 chopped red peppers, seeds and membrane removed (optional, but nice)

Place all ingredients in a pot and simmer uncovered at least 2 hours, or until sauce has thickened, STIRRING FREQUENTLY. Pour into pint jars. If you want to shelve them, sterilize the jars and process in a boiling water bath, or just refrigerate.

Playing With Your Food

Fire:
It seems like it's doing nothing forever, and then suddenly, all the liquid has evaporated, so make sure to check on it, especially near the end.

Basil Pesto

Yields about 1 ½ cups pesto

2 cloves garlic

1/4 cup pine nuts

2 -3 cups basil leaves, packed

1/3-1/2 cup freshly grated parmesan cheese (not the processed kind)

1/2 - 3/4 cup olive oil

Salt to taste

In a food processor, purée garlic and pine nuts into a thick paste. Add basil and parmesan cheese, process until smooth. Keep the food processor going and pour olive oil in a slow stream until pesto has desired consistency. Add salt if necessary (the parmesan is salty)

To freeze:

Put individual servings in ice cube trays or put small amounts in ziploc bags so you can defrost just the amount you need

Serve over anything.

Playing With Your Food

Guests:

Everybody loves pesto. You can serve it room temperature on pasta. You can put it on crackers. Buy a pizza dough, spread it on the dough and bake it for a quick meal, or cut up as snacks. Add a piece of fresh tomato and it's a gourmet snack.

Substitutions:

Walnuts instead of pine nuts

Half basil, half parsley

Or you can use arugula instead of basil

1/2 Parmesan, 1/2 Romano

Oops:

There is a lot of leeway in quantity as you can see. Some people like it cheesy, some people like strong basil flavor, and some people like it runny. However, be aware of your garlic. I once thought, I LOVE garlic, let me put a ton in! I put in about 6 cloves of garlic. The result was a shocking experience that took another harvest of basil to repair! Other than that, feel free to experiment, the worst that can happen is you end up with something you add vinegar to as salad dressing.

Asian Basil Pesto

This is a variation when you're sick of cheese and pine nuts.

1 tablespoon peeled, chopped ginger root

1 –2 small jalapeño peppers, seeded

1/4 cup lightly toasted peanuts or 1/2 cup cooked white beans (two complete different flavors but they both work)

1 1/2 cups packed fresh basil

1/2 cup cilantro leaves

107

1 tablespoon peanut oil

1 tablespoon toasted sesame oil

1/3 – 1/2 cup water

Salt and pepper to taste

Place ginger, jalapeños, and peanuts or beans in food processor. Pulse until coarsely chopped. Add basil, cilantro, oils and 1/3 cup water; purée. If it's too thick for you, add water. Salt and pepper to taste.

You can serve this with cooked noodles, brown rice or just add some to a stir fry.

Playing With Your Food

Substitutions:
You can leave out the cilantro
If you leave out the jalapeños, it's a milder version

Oops:
If you overcook or undercook the white beans, it's OK, it all goes into the mix!

Fire:
If you're toasting the peanuts, make sure to shake the pan and keep an eye on them.

Aioli Sauce

Makes about a cup

This is basically a garlic mayonnaise with a fancy name. It is awesome on grilled vegetables, as a dip for steamed artichokes, or in the middle of a vegetarian antipasto platter.

4 cloves peeled garlic

1 egg yolk, room temperature (to bring an egg to room temperature quickly, place it in a bowl of hot water)

Salt and freshly ground white (or black) pepper to taste

Juice of half a lemon (about 2 tablespoons)

1/2 teaspoon Dijon mustard

3/4 cup oil (half olive, half peanut is ideal)

Purée garlic in food processor. Whisk the egg yolk until light and smooth and add to the garlic. Add salt and pepper to taste, lemon juice and mustard and process to a smooth paste.

With the machine running pour the oil very slowly into the mixture in a steady stream, blending constantly. Continue blending until you obtain a thick, shiny, firm sauce, like mayonnaise. Refrigerate till ready to use.

Playing With Your Food

Substitutions:
This mayonnaise and the one on page _____ are both good basic ways to make any number of mayonnaises. Add basil, take out some garlic, add chipotle or roasted red pepper purée, the possibilities are endless.

Oops:
As mentioned before, if it doesn't work, use it as dressing or start over. It's not the end of the world.

Fresh Italian Tomato Sauce
Serves 4

I once came back from traveling. Not wanting to hassle with a complex meal, I thought I'd defrost some of this sauce for a quick meal. In the freezer I found a note from my housesitter. "I hope you don't mind. One night I got hungry and thought I'd heat up a little of your sauce to put on the pasta. The next thing I knew, it was gone. It was the best pasta sauce I've ever eaten. I'd love the recipe." Well Lauren, here it is.

1/4 cup olive oil

2 medium onions, chopped

3 – 4 cloves of garlic minced or chopped (it depends if you want the flavor evenly distributed or you like to bite into chunks of garlic)

1 sweet red pepper, seeded and chopped

12 – 15 fresh plum tomatoes, peeled, seeded (see page 58) and coarsely chopped

1 tablespoon tomato paste

9 pitted Kalamata olives, chopped in quarters

1 tablespoon capers

1/3 cup red wine

1 large bay leaf

1 tablespoon dried or 3 tablespoons chopped, fresh oregano

1/2 teaspoon fennel seeds

2 teaspoons salt

1/2 teaspoon freshly ground pepper

1/4 cup fresh basil, finely chopped

Heat oil over medium low heat. Add onions and sauté till just getting soft. Add the garlic, sauté about 2 minutes more. Add the red peppers and cook for about 2 more minutes. Add all the other ingredients except the basil. Cover and simmer, stirring occasionally until the tomatoes break down and the sauce begins to thicken, about 45 minutes. After that, you can remove the lid, add the basil and cook the sauce down to your desired thickness. You may want to add more salt and pepper at the end to your taste.

Playing With Your Food

Substitutions:

You can use canned plum tomatoes. The flavor is different, and you may find you have to use a (perish the thought) touch of sugar to balance the tartness.

Mushrooms, carrots, eggplant could all be added when you add the tomatoes. Or add chopped zucchini at the end.

If you have no fresh basil, but there's some frozen pesto on hand, throw a couple of tablespoons in.

If you have no tomato paste, it still tastes fine, just might need a little more time to thicken. No red wine? Use white, or skip it, it will be fine.

Meat eaters can add meatballs, ground meat or sausage to the sauce.

No bay leaf? No one will know.

Oops:

If you accidentally throw the basil in with the rest of the ingredients, it won't harm the recipe. The basil taste just won't be as strong.

Fire:

It's good to keep an eye on the sauce near the end, since it can start to stick to the pan.

D ESSERTS

Seize the moment. Remember all those women on the Titanic
who waved off the dessert cart.
— Erma Bombeck

Stressed spelled backwards is desserts. Coincidence?
I think not!
— Author Unknown

The Food of Paradise
Persian Folk Tale

Long ago, in what was even then called the city of Baghdad, a mullah named Nasrudin was pondering the nature of God. "Why do I have to work and teach and grovel for my daily sustenance?" he asked himself. "Is it not written that God will provide for all who have faith?"

Finally, he decided to prove this once and for all. Nasrudin left Baghdad to wander the countryside. Each day, he waited for God to provide him with what was needed to stay alive. But nothing happened.

"I'm just not pious enough," was his first thought. After all, he didn't pray as much as he could, his faith was a little weak. Even now, he was entertaining serious doubts about his plan. He imagined the bowl of steaming porridge he'd be eating right now at his home and started to really regret his decision.

He finally arrived at the bank of a river, exhausted, famished, and defeated. He hurled himself down and went to sleep, convinced he'd never make it back home. The next morning he was awakened by sunbeams. He looked out on the river. Floating towards him was a packet, something wrapped in leaves. Could it be?

The Mullah reached and grabbed the packet as it floated towards him. Trembling, he unwrapped it. Oh delight! It was the most delicious halva, crushed nuts, honey, attar of roses – absolute ambrosia! He ate it with gusto, and marveled at the power of God.

The next day another packet appeared. Each day, he was sustained by this heavenly halva. But he could no longer remain on the bank. He wanted to find the source of this blessed gift. Each day he traveled further upstream trying to track the package. Then one day, he came upon a magnificent castle. As he stared at it, a beautiful woman leaned out and tossed a package into the river.

So that was it! The food of the gods was delivered to the Mullah by the hand of a gorgeous princess. The Mullah could not believe his good fortune. He rushed to the castle and insisted on an audience with the princess. She was more beautiful than he could even have imagined. "To what do I owe this blessed visit, most holy man?" the princess inquired.

"Oh, no, it is I who am indebted to you, fair princess!" The Mullah fell to his knees and prostrated himself. The princess was puzzled. "I don't understand."

"Ah, you are too humble, fair Princess," cried the Mullah. "You think I don't know that it is your very hand that each day tossed the heavenly halva out your window which has sustained me all these weeks!"

"Halva?" The Princess was puzzled, then suddenly blushed. "What I was tossing out the window was what was left over from my bath. Each day I rub myself with almonds, honey and fragrances. Then I scrape it off, pack it together and throw it out the window!"

"Ah, now I see!" cried Nasrudin. "God does truly provide food for all, but its quality and kind are dictated by what the man deserves!"

The Killer Carrot Cake

(indebted to the *Silver Palate Cookbook*)

Serves at least 10

3 cups unbleached all purpose flour

3 cups granulated sugar

1 teaspoon salt

1 tablespoon baking soda

1 tablespoon ground cinnamon

1 1/2 cups corn oil

4 large eggs, lightly beaten

1 tablespoon vanilla extract

1 1/2 cups shelled walnuts, chopped

1 1/2 cups shredded coconut

1 1/3 cups puréed cooked carrots (about 2 1/2 carrots)

3/4 drained crushed pineapple

Preheat oven to 350 degrees. Grease two 9-inch springform pans. If you don't have these, you can use round cake pans, grease them and then flour them by putting some flour in the pan, then tilting and turning the pan till it's covered with a uniform dusting of flour.

Sift dry ingredients into a bowl. Add oil, eggs and vanilla. Beat well. Fold in walnuts, coconut, carrots and pineapple.

Pour batter into the prepared pans. Set on the middle rack of the oven and bake for 50 minutes, until edges have pulled away from sides and a cake tester (a knife does very nicely) inserted in center comes out clean. Don't be upset if the cake doesn't seem very high. By the time you stack the layers and add the icing, it's very impressive. Let it cool a little before removing from the pan.

Cool on a cake rack for 2 hours. Fill cake and frost sides with cream cheese frosting.

Cream Cheese Frosting:

8 oz. cream cheese, at room temperature

6 tablespoons unsalted butter, at room temperature

1 cup sifted confectioner's sugar

1 teaspoon vanilla extract

Juice of 1/2 lemon (optional, adds a nice tang)

or

1/2 teaspoon orange zest (optional)

or 1 tablespoon Cointreau or Grand Marnier (optional)

Cream together cream cheese and butter in a mixing bowl. Slowly sift in confectioner's sugar and continue beating until fully incorporated. Mixture should be free of lumps.

Note: I use less sugar than the original recipe calls for. It doesn't hurt the texture at all, but it does affect the amount of icing you end up with. Since you are adding slowly, feel free to taste it and decide on your sweetness level.

Stir in vanilla and other ingredients you choose to use.

Playing With Your Food

Guests:

This is a spectacular dessert that has never had leftovers at a party. But it's a big cake. You can halve the ingredients and have a lovely dessert for 4 – 6 people.

Substitutions:

You can use puréed fresh or frozen pineapple. The only problem is that if you try to drain it, you end up with nothing, and if you keep all the liquid, it makes the cake take longer to bake.

Oops:

I've forgotten that the cake needs to cool before icing it, and guests were already at the door. As long as it's not burning hot, you should be fine. Alternatively, you can have everything ready, then invite your guests to ice the cake after dinner! Tell them it's the new, interactive dinner party.

Fire:

Depending on your oven, the cake may take a little longer or shorter to bake. If when you take it out, it appears you have burnt some of the outside, just gently slice it off and cover it with icing – no one will ever know.
(Unless of course, you haven't iced it yet!)

Peach Cobbler
Serves 4

4 -5 cups peeled and sliced ripe peaches

2/3 cups plus 3 tablespoons sugar

1 teaspoon grated lemon zest

1 tablespoon lemon juice

1/4 teaspoon almond extract

1 1/2 cups unbleached all purpose flour

1 tablespoon baking powder

1/2 teaspoon salt

1/3 cup vegetable shortening or butter

1 egg, lightly beaten

1/4 cup milk

Topping:

1 cup heavy cream

3 -4 tablespoons peach brandy or peach cordial

Note on peaches: Peaches shrink a lot when they cook. The first time I made this dessert, it seemed like the peaches were completely overwhelmed by the dough. If you like a more fruity dessert, pile in some more peaches, but use the same size baking pan. You may or may not want to add more sugar if you add peaches. You can also put less dough on your cobbler.

Preheat oven to 400 degrees. Butter a 2-quart baking dish.

Arrange peaches in baking dish. Sprinkle with 2/3 cup sugar, the lemon zest and juice, and almond extract. They disappear under the dough, so don't worry about arranging them aesthetically, they can be on top of each other.   Bake for 20 minutes.

While peaches are baking, sift flour, 1 tablespoon of the remaining sugar, the baking powder and salt together into a bowl. Cut in shortening until mixture resembles cornmeal. You can do the above in a food processor as well, but if you are using butter, cut it into small chunks, then pulse the processor. Otherwise, just use your fingers. Combine beaten egg and milk and mix into dry ingredients until JUST COMBINED. Don't over mix.

Remove peaches from oven and quickly drop dough by large spoonfuls over surface. The blobs will spread out and puff, so if you don't like a lot of crust, here's where you can decide on amounts. Sprinkle with remaining 2 tablespoons of sugar. Return to the oven for 15 - 20 minutes, until top is firm and golden brown.

For topping - whip cream to soft peaks. (If you chill your beaters in the freezer before whipping, success is guaranteed.) Flavor with peach brandy to taste. Or just serve it with a scoop of your favorite vanilla ice cream.

Playing With Your Food

Substitutions:
You can make this a berry cobbler. Just add a tablespoon of corn starch and a teaspoon of cinnamon to the berries before baking. If the berries are tart, don't add lemon juice. For an interesting flavor "zing" add 1 teaspoon grated fresh ginger or 1/4 teaspoon dried ginger to the peaches before baking.
 If you don't have almond extract, it's just fine.
You certainly don't need the peach brandy in the whipped cream.

Oops:
One of the biggest mistakes new cooks make is over-mixing the dough. There's that moment of doubt, "this can't possibly be enough, it should be smooth," etc., etc. The more you beat it, the less life it has, so err on the side of less.

I can't tell you how many times I just poured all the sugar in the recipe into the peaches instead of reserving that bit for the dough, or forgot to add sugar to the biscuit dough, or forgot to sprinkle sugar on top of the dough. No one will know but you – it still turns out fine.

Chocolate Pecan Pie

(no calories of course)

Serves 12

Crust :This amount is for an 11 inch tart pan. If you are doing a 9-inch pie, you can reduce by 1/3, or just make the whole batch and have a thicker crust. It is, in either case, a slightly thicker crust than a fruit pie.

2 cups unbleached flour

1 tablespoon sugar

Pinch of salt

1 3/4 sticks unsalted butter, cut into small pieces

1/4 cup cold (ice) water

(around 2 cups of dried lentils, peas or rice for weighing down the crust)

Filling:

3 extra large eggs

1 cup light corn syrup or sugar syrup (see note)

1 stick unsalted better, melted

5 oz. semisweet chocolate morsels or 5 oz. semisweet chocolate, melted

1 1/2 cups pecans, toasted for 10 minutes in a preheated 350 degree oven

1/4 cup dark rum

1/8 teaspoon salt

Note: This recipe harks from the days when high fructose corn syrup seemed like the elixir of life. Since then, it has fallen out of favor and may, by this printing, even be politically incorrect. To make 1 cup of sugar syrup, bring 3/4 cup of water to a boil. Add 1 cup sugar and stir till sugar is dissolved. Continue cooking for a few minutes, stirring constantly till it begins to thicken and has reduced slightly (to about 1 cup).

Crust:

Preheat the oven to 450 degrees. Put flour, sugar and salt into the food processor. Pulse a few seconds. Add butter, pulse several times till it's mixed in and has the texture of corn meal. Add water a little at a time, till absorbed. You can also use your fingers as mentioned on pg. ____. Roll it out gently, do not overwork it, and press it into a pie pan. Gently press dough into sides of pan to prevent shrinkage. Prick the bottom of the crust with a fork and finish the edges with a pie crust trim. Line the shell with aluminum foil. Make sure you cover the edges on top. Fill it with the dried beans or rice to weigh it down. Bake in the oven for 8 – 10 minutes, until edges are slightly browned. (You might have to pick up the aluminum foil a bit to peek.) Remove the pan from the oven.

Lower the oven temperature to 375 degrees.

Carefully remove the beans or rice and foil. Return the pan to the oven and bake for 5 minutes more, or until the crust is slightly opaque and less moist. At this point it is important to poke air out of any large blisters which may have risen in the crust. Remove from the oven and set aside.

Lower the oven temperature to 350 degrees.

While the crust is baking, combine all the filling ingredients in a medium-size mixing bowl. Pour the filling into the pre-baked pie shell and bake for 35 – 45 minutes. Check it after 35 minutes, don't let it over cook. There will still be a tiny bit of bubbling, but it won't be liquid. If you wait till the whole thing is dark and solid, it's like a rock when it cools. Allow the pie to cool completely before serving.

Note: Using a tart pan is brave . You have to remember to loosen the crust from the edges; if your crust has baked over the top of the pan, sometimes it gets stuck. Then, once you've lifted it out of the mold, you have to find a way to slide the darn thing onto a plate. I've often just given up and left the bottom of the tart pan on the pie, which then can get ruined when you cut. You can carefully slide a metal spatula in between the pie and the base, and SLOWLY slide it. It looks absolutely beautiful. But if you are just serving pieces and not doing a presentation, I say, just use a pie pan!

Playing With Your Food

Guests:
This pie is so rich that you can get up to 15 pieces out of it.

Oops:
In trying to get the pie off the tart pan, I've broken it in half. One time the crust fell off one section. Another time, somehow the dough welded itself to the pan. In all of those instances, I've not "presented" the pie, and just served the pieces with ice cream.

Fire:
Blind pre-baking a crust can seem scary the first couple of times. If you just stick with these instructions and temperatures, you'll succeed every time. Use an oven timer, don't trust your
"inner clock."
It is critical to not overcook the pie with the filling.

Are We Having Fun Yet?
The only real mistake is the one from which we learn nothing.
— John Powell
I stand by all the misstatements that I've made.
— Dan Quayle

About 20 years ago, I decided North Jersey needed a summer performing arts festival. Why should we be a province of New York City? It would be affordable, excellent entertainment under the night sky. In the spirit of Judy Garland and Mickey Rooney, we built a stage (if you build it they will come, right?), made signs, sent press releases, hired performers. I did it all with my own money, because I was too impatient to apply for a grant. And besides, how could we fail?

That summer, every weekend a show was scheduled, it rained. We tried rain dates, but people got confused or couldn't come a second time. Some performers were flexible, many were not, and insisted on being paid anyway. Once it even rained on the rain date. The expensive rented lights were constantly being covered and uncovered, occasionally breaking. We all soon excelled at grabbing ladders and scrambling with tarps at stupidly precarious heights. At the blessed end of the debacle season, I was so in debt, it took years to recover.

My friend Nancy, a nurse with vision, did something similar. Long before Holistic Health Fairs were ubiquitous, she conceived a huge event, a model festival that could have been the template for the ones we see today. The day of the fair, there was a huge blizzard. Nancy lost everything, had to re-finance her house and start again. Which she did. When we talked, she shrugged, "You never know when AFGO will hit you."

"AFGO?"

"Another F*&$%ing Growth Opportunity. It's a nursing term."

One year I was hiking in New England with my sister Liz, who was going through an "unhappy" phase. "Well," I said in my best 'I'm evolved and you're not' voice, "It's about practice, and studying yourself. Think of this as a learning experience." She held her arms aloft, fists clenched. Surely, someone coming to the top of the mountain, seeing her backlit against the reddening sky would have interpreted a posture of triumph at accomplishing the summit. But instead she screamed, "I am SO sick of learning about myself! I just want to be done!"

Somewhere in our wiring, we have been convinced that learning must be painful. Blundering through life, I embark on projects, get involved in relationships, and meddle in others' business, only to learn later that perhaps there was another way. Still, I learn, lick my wounds and move on.

Feldenkrais often said, "Learning should be a pleasurable experience. If you're not having fun, you're not learning." In the movement classes, we constantly check in on the pleasure principle. If it hurts, don't do it. If there is resistance, wait. If a movement is impossible, imagine it. And above all, rest. Feldenkrais proposed that learning under pressure or with pain produces compulsion. Fancy that.

I now recognize that my brief career as a summer festival producer was laden with compulsions.

First, my delusions of grandeur: "I could be the NJ version of Joseph Papp! We will conquer the world of theater!"

Second, it was a counter-phobic strategy. I was so uptight about auditioning for roles in NYC and getting rejected, that I thought producing an entire festival would be easier. Kind of like buying a new house because the refrigerator is broken.

Third, misplaced affection. I was also still trying in some way to make my father, who no longer even lived in NJ and certainly knows nothing about theater, proud of me.

By not paying attention to small details like weather, I became a poster child for Self-Saboteurs Anonymous. After all, it rains every weekend in the summer in NJ, it's a karmic thing. Nancy could have avoided her AFGO simply by waiting till spring to hold her event. Sure, neither one of us wanted to admit we were wrong. It's so easy to blame the weather. We learned, as my father would say, the hard way.

A survey was once conducted among successful and failed neurosurgeons. When asked to describe their mistakes, the successful surgeons spoke candidly about errors in judgment, the learning that took place and how they improved as a result. The failed surgeons; which included people who had dropped out of medical school, had lost their licenses or had switched careers, all blamed someone else. The nurse, bad lighting, the patient's attitude. Not one of them acknowledged the possibility that he had made a mistake. In a Feldenkrais lesson, we are often *encouraged* to make mistakes, to intentionally do things badly. Feldenkrais often said that it's better to *know* you are doing something badly, than to compulsively try to do a good job.

There is an alchemical formula, "As above, so below." The alchemists believed that humans are little universes. And that the universe is a sentient being, evolving and learning alongside us. As we expand, it does too. I wonder: does it follow the pleasure principle or is there compulsion involved? Does it follow a recipe for creating a star system, or does it just throw some ingredients together? Are supernovas intentional, or a kitchen disaster? We are told that supernovas spew out the materials that form planets and ultimately, humans. I eavesdrop on the cosmic conversation.

"Wahoo! What a cosmic feast this will be!"

Or "Oops, guess I should have turned the temperature down a little earlier."

Or maybe, "Oh no, I've gone too far! AFGO!"

Is it possible that what I consider to be a mistake is just part of the plan? After all, without supernovas, we wouldn't exist.

Then again, maybe we are a mistake. In the *Cyberiad* by Stanislaus Lem, two robots named Klaupacious and Trull are responsible for creation and maintenance of one sector of the universe. The cosmic equivalent of Laurel and Hardy, they bungle countless evolutionary processes and blow up dozens of star systems. For eons, they dump their debris on a small piece of lifeless rock. Imagine their embarrassment when they are informed that the junk they have deposited has accidentally developed a consciousness, resulting in a bizarre creature that has named its planet Earth.

If I go slowly, pay attention to where the resistance is and don't try to accomplish, perhaps instead of painful learning, I can enjoy the process. I may see the fear of failure, or the distractions that lead to my burnt sauce, or overcooked vegetables. Feldenkrais said, "If you know what you are doing, you can do what you want." He also said, "It doesn't matter whether you do it well or badly, as long as you *know* you're doing it badly!" Acknowledging my AFGO and learning to love my mistakes is an excellent place for learning, and where better than in the kitchen, where you can just wipe everything up and start from scratch.

Tart Tatin

Serves 10 – 12

This spectacular, easy (but time consuming) pie is the ultimate testimonial to loving your mistakes. It is the result of a kitchen disaster in the Tatin sisters' kitchen. Accidentally burning the apples, they improvised the following dessert and made pastry history. I love to make this with a whole bunch of different kinds of apples during apple harvest season. However, you can make it with any kind you want – the original recipe I used called for Golden Delicious. You also need a 10-inch cast iron skillet, or some other oven proof skillet.

10 – 12 apples

7–8 tablespoons butter

1/3 cup plus 3 tablespoons sugar

1 tablespoon lemon juice or water

1 sheet of puff pastry dough (you can buy it in the frozen section of your supermarket) or 1 recipe of the pie dough from the previous recipe for Chocolate Pecan Pie.

Whipped cream, crème fraiche or ice cream (optional)

Peel, halve and core the apples. With the cut side down, trim a sliver off of one side of each half, so that the apples can stand on their sides. I like to then place them into the skillet, so that I know how many apples I really need as I'm going along, since apples often vary in size. You will have to remove them for the next step if you measure like this.

Heat the skillet on medium/low heat. Melt the butter, add the sugar and lemon juice (if apples are sweet) or water (if apples are tart) and mix well. The sugar will not be totally dissolved, just heading in that direction.

Starting at the outside of the pan put the apples in a circle, on their sides, one right up against the other, so they look like a wreath. Once you've got the outer circle, put two halves facing each other in the middle. Then fit more apples in wherever you can till it's as tight as you can get it. Don't worry if it doesn't look aesthetically perfect, it will later!

Let them cook slowly. You may even have to lower the flame. It will take about a half hour for the apples to sink and shrink. Meanwhile, preheat the oven to 425 degrees.

If you have cut too much apple, as they cook, you can stick more pieces in the gaps. You'll know the apples are done when your sugar mixture bubbles slowly and is a rich, dark brown. If it's starting to brown early, turn your stove down even more.

Put the whole skillet in the oven for 5 minutes, then remove it. (Use a potholder!) Turn the oven up to 475 degrees.

Roll out your dough so it's big enough to drape over your skillet. Lay it right on top, then with a knife, quickly cut the dough off the edge. It will sink into your skillet. Put it in the oven for 15 - 20 minutes, till the crust is slightly brown. Remove.

Run a knife around the inside of the skillet to separate any apples that stuck to the edge. Take a heat-proof dish and place it on top of the crust. Flip the pan over onto the plate. SLLLOOOWWLY lift the skillet. You may want to have a spatula handy to help scrape off any stuck apple. Stick those pieces back into the tart like pieces in a puzzle. Then take your knife or spatula and kind of push the apples toward the center a bit, and smooth everything down on top.

It's best served warm and re-heats beautifully.

Playing With Your Food

Guests:

When it comes out nicely, this is definitely a "bring it to the table to cut" pie. However, sometimes the apples don't all come out of the pan perfectly, so use your own aesthetics in presenting. I find it so delicious, it really doesn't need cream, etc, but it certainly adds even more delight to the dessert. Again, it's extremely rich so a little goes a long way.

Oops:

You have to work fast once you lay the dough on. I've had pieces break and just threw them into the pan, and they all melted together into a lovely crust.

I've forgotten to add the water and had no damage.

Don't panic if your apples are stuck to the pan when you try to unmold it. It's no big deal to scrape them up and stick it into the tart. But as noted above, if all else fails, serve the good pieces to your guests, save the rest for yourself!

Fire:

It is important to watch the color of the sugar as it's cooking on top. It seems like it's doing nothing forever, then suddenly turns brown.

You have to really be ready when laying the dough on because it softens really quickly on top of the apples.

Don't forget to use a potholder!

LAYING IN THE KITCHEN

Russian Tea Cakes
Makes about 35 balls

So, these are not cakes but cookies. They are also called Mexican wedding cakes, Polish divorce cookies and Swedish Christmas cookies, so the Russian part is dubious. However, they do taste great with tea! They are easy, delicious and keep forever, OK up to a month.

1 cup softened butter
1 cup powdered sugar (plus more for topping)
1 1/2 teaspoons vanilla
2 1/4 cups all purpose flour
1 cup finely chopped pecans (feel free to coarsely grind in the food processor!)
3/4 teaspoon salt

Heat oven to 350 degrees. Mix butter, 1 cup of powdered sugar and the vanilla till creamy. Stir in flour, nuts and salt and blend until dough holds together. Shape into 1 inch balls. Place about 1 inch apart on ungreased cookie sheets. Bake for 17 - 20 minutes or until set but not brown. Roll in powdered sugar while warm. Cool. If desired, roll in powdered sugar again.

Playing With Your Food

Guests: This is perfect for a party where people are milling and dancing and want to pop something sweet into their mouths. And you can make the cookies way in advance!

Substitutions:

Walnuts instead of pecans work fine.

Oops:

Don't stress about the exact size of the balls, although you don't want them too big.

Fire:

One thing about cookies, they're done when they still don't look done. Once they're brown on top, they're over done. If you feel insecure, check the bottom of a cookie. If the bottom is light brown, they're done! They'll firm up as they cool.

Attitude Adjustment

There are people who come to see me because an ordinary household task has become unbearably painful: folding the laundry, washing windows, doing the dishes. Occasionally they speak resentfully, calling the activity a boring, mundane responsibility. There's a Zen saying, "Before enlightenment, chop wood, carry water. After enlightenment, chop wood, carry water." Everything in life can be approached with a spirit of play or an attitude of drudgery. I recently read an article about a rock star, living a glamorous life many of us would envy, who complained about the routine of standing in front of 10,000 people and singing their hit songs. It's not what you do, it's how you do it.

Pleasure and pain are two of our primitive response mechanisms. Both of them trigger emotions in us. And our emotions can often change our somatic experience. Washing dishes after having cooked dinner for a new lover can make you want to sing, while sitting through the most exquisite symphony after hearing your novel's been rejected can be a miserable experience.

Thinking, feeling, sensing and movement are always happening, one always affecting the other. By noticing your posture, i.e. your physical attitude, you can often adjust your mental or emotional attitude. You can also relieve physical discomfort simply by exploring options around how you stand and move.

Sometimes you just have to give yourself some new ways of moving. If throughout your life you've washed dishes bent over the sink, head jutting slightly forward, back tense and arms doing all the work, it's difficult to be comfortable, and enjoyment becomes elusive. The following exploration is something you can try

130

henever you need an attitude adjustment. In addition to helping your posture, practicing this exploration will make dishwashing easier; and you may discover that you can look at the world a little differently.

You can do this standing by the sink or a counter or even sitting down. If you need support while standing, you can rest your hands on the counter or sink.

Begin by taking a comfortable stance and notice your posture. Where are your shoulders in relation to your ears? Do they feel rounded? Pulled back? Resting easily? How does your neck feel? Your low back? Are your knees locked? Loose? Are your toes gripping? Curled up? Relaxed? What is your breathing like?

Slowly, begin lowering your head down toward your chest. Then just as slowly, raise your head to look up to the ceiling. Do you feel movement anywhere else as you do this? In your neck? Your chest? Your low back? Don't try to force a movement, just notice the experience. Do the movement four or five times, then pause. If you are finding this tiring, grab a chair or stool and take a seated rest.

Take a fresh stance. Repeat the movements of the head, but this time, exhale each time you lower your head and inhale as you raise it. As you breathe, can you let your chest move? As your head goes down, let your back round a bit. As you look up, arch your back and let the front of your chest expand. Allow your knees to bend slightly. Let your arms just hang naturally (unless you are holding on to the sink). Repeat this four or five times, then take another rest.

Take a fresh stance. This time, as you lower your head, bend your knees as much as is comfortable and pull your belly in towards your spine, rounding your entire back. Let your arms dangle. Don't bend so far that your arms go below your knees. Inhale as you move back to your regular standing posture and on the next exhale, raise your head, arch your back and push your belly forward. Yes, I really mean exhale, and I really mean push your belly out. Make sure you don't "lock" your knees back as you arch.

Americans seem to think that a flat stomach is sexy. But as I mentioned in the first exercise in this book, your power center is located in your belly. Walking around trying to hold your stomach in all the time is like holding back your power center. There are complex muscular relationships between your stomach and your back and when you continually hold your stomach in, your back muscles will suffer. You want to find the balance in the muscular work between front and back. Intentionally protruding your belly as you arch in this exercise can help you regain some of that balance. Try rounding and arching a few times. Now notice your posture. Take a walk around the kitchen. What does washing dishes feel like now?

Conclusion

Many people finish a meal with an after dinner drink, a cup of tea or coffee. In simpler times, men retired to the smoking room to have cigars and the women sat in the parlor to chat. Often the conversation was the result of the meal; its quality, the amount or variety. The real intention of course, was to digest. At the end of every Feldenkrais lesson, students are invited to walk around and notice how they are feeling. They "digest" the material and often, before heading out the door, chat about their experience.

I hope this book has provided you with some conversation pieces as you digest the material, and that all your functions; thinking, feeling, sensing and moving, feel well-fed. In Poland, as each person stands to leave the table, he says, "Thank you." And I thank you.

Acknowledgments

First to the many people who asked for this book, and who insisted that Feldenkrais lessons were the perfect garnish for a meal, thanks for all your support. This book would not be possible without my husband Ron, who besides providing the cover photos, has sampled and critiqued every dish and has suffered as my sous-chef for over 30 years. My writers' group in Asheville; Carole King, Laura Facciponti, Barbara Marlowe and Bonita Osley all provided insightful feedback, ideas and support. Allen Tucker heroically read the first draft of this book and helped immeasurably with titles, amounts, and pithy observations. The editors of Western North Carolina Magazine, Julie Parker and Sandi Tomlin-Sutker first published several of the essays included in this book, and I am grateful to have such a supportive place to develop my writing. To the many friends and relatives who tried the recipes in the manuscript and called me with questions like: "It says add the basil, but you don't have basil in the ingredients," or "You ask for 8 oz. of tofu, but then the filling only fills half the pie," or "Are you sure you really mean 1/2 cup of cumin?", there's no greater compliment than knowing that people are carefully reading the recipe!

Glossary

Agave Syrup – a sweet syrup that comes from the Agave plant (the same plant that gives us tequila). It's lower in carbs, while maintaining sweetness and mixes well in cold things, better than honey or sugar. Available in health food stores.

Arborio Rice – An Italian rice that has fatter grains than our traditional white rice. It's generally used for risotto. You can find it in any gourmet store, or many super-markets.

Asafetida powder – This spice is actually the source of our English word Fetid. And what a smell! If you are not going to cook Indian food often, you can easily skip this spice. But it adds such a pungent flavor, and it's cheap, so if you want to experiment, go for it. I recommend after you buy it to make sure you store it in a tightly sealed jar. Indian grocery stores and online.

Bulgur Wheat – This is a quick-cooking form of whole wheat that has been cleaned, parboiled, dried, ground into particles and sifted into distinct sizes. Since it's pre-cooked, you just have to soak it. The different grinds offer an interesting tex-ture. While we traditionally think of it only in tabbouleh, there are many Middle Eastern recipes like pilaf that use bulgur wheat. Most supermarkets carry bulgur, but you can definitely find it in a health food store.
Chick Pea Flour – Also called GRAM in Indian and Asian stores,
Garam Masala – this just means spice mixture. Every Indian family has their own version. You can find it in any Indian grocery store. I actually saw that McCormicks now makes a garam masala and sells it in the spice section of the supermarket.

Ghee – is nothing more than clarified butter. You can make it yourself, but it's read-ily available in Indian grocery stores and some health food stores. It's a staple of In-dian cooking and keeps in your refrigerator for a really long time.

Miso – is fermented soybean paste. Sounds gruesome but it's a delicious staple in Japanese cooking and has many flavors and varieties. White miso is almost sweet. Each type of miso has a different quality – great to add to broths or spreads for a unique flavor. Miso is sold in most health food and Asian specialty stores.

Phyllo Dough – is very thin sheets of dough that is used for dishes ranging from Greek spinach pie to apple streudel. You can find it in the freezer section of the supermarket where you buy pie crust and other frozen doughs.

Pomegranate Molasses – You can find this in most Middle Eastern Grocery Stores. It keeps forever and adds an unusual sweet tang to recipes.

Quinoa – (pronounced keen-wah) – comes from the Andes and can be used as a grain or wheat substitute in many recipes. It has a distinct nutty flavor and is easy to cook. Sold in health food stores.

Seitan (pronounced see-tan) is wheat gluten – the protein of wheat. While you can make it yourself, it is very time consuming and readily available both in health food stores and Asian grocery stores – where you'll find it sold as "Vegetarian Chicken or Duck."

Tahini – is a paste made of sesame seeds. You can buy it in a can at the supermarket. Many health food stores sell it in their bulk section

Tamari Sauce – a Japanese soy sauce that has little to no wheat and a rich flavor.

Tamarind Juice – is right up there with Pomegranate Molasses. You'll use it once or twice a year. It's a sweet tang that can be omitted, or substituted. Available at Asian grocery stores.

Tempeh – is a fermented soy bean cake. It is often mixed with a grain or vegetables to improve its flavor. While on its own, it's an "acquired" taste, there are many ways to improve its flavor and it is an excellent source of vegetarian protein. Available in health food stores.

Tofu – While most people now know what tofu is at this point, there is confusion on the types. Chinese-style tofu is spongy and good for stir fry or deep frying. Silken tofu can be used in pies and desserts, often you can't tell the difference between a silken tofu pie and one made with cream cheese. All are sold in supermarkets.

Resources

Books

Irma S. Rombauer, Marion Becker Rombauer, Ethan Becker, *Joy of Cooking* (New York: Scribner, 2007)

Yamuna Devi, *Lord Krishna's Cuisine* (New York: Penguin-Putnam, 1987)

Julee Rosso, Sheila Lukins, *The Silver Palate Cookbook* (New York: Workman Publishing Company, 2007)

Moshe Feldenkrais, *Awareness through Movement* (New York: Harper One, 1991)

Lavinia Plonka, *What Are You Afraid Of? A Body/Mind Guide to Courageous Living* (New York: Penguin, 2003)

Lavinia Plonka, *Walking Your Talk: Changing Your Life through the Magic of Body Language* (New York: Penguin, 2006)

Websites

Recipe Ideas

Vegetariantimes.com

Epicurious.com

Cooks.com

Purchasing Ingredients

Ethnicfoodsco.com

Asianfoodgrocer.com

Thespicehouse.com

Body/Mind

feldenkrais.com

laviniaplonka.com

achievingexcellence.com – a website selling CDs and books about Feldenkrais